M.O.M.S.

A 12-Step Guide for Mothers of Married Sons

M. Margaret West

To my sons -- I have loved you since before you were born. You have enriched my life beyond words.

Preface

Mothers-in-law have long been fodder for comedic talk-show host monologues. They've been despised, ridiculed, dismissed, shunned and barely tolerated. Myriad jokes and word play circulate across the internet. Letters spelling "mother-in-law," when rearranged, spell "Woman Hitler." Funny? You decide. Perhaps some of this behavior is warranted, but I venture to suggest that the majority of mothers-in-law have just been gravely misunderstood – especially mothers of sons.

I never gave mothers of married sons much thought. I knew my husband, Michael, had a mother and I even liked her – a lot. We saw each other on most major holidays, I sent greeting cards on her birthday, Easter, Mother's Day, Halloween and Valentine's Day and I chatted with her on the phone whenever she called. Edna was part of my extended family, but in no way was she an active participant in my daily life. She was very much on the periphery of my little world. During Girls' Nights Out with my girlfriends, I'd listen as others complained about how intrusive, needy, demanding and judgmental their mothers-in-law were! I never had any similar negative experiences to contribute or venom to spew that included me in this group of victims of monsters-in-law. I felt very lucky – lucky indeed – to have the perfect mother-in-law – one that I kept at a distance -- not by design, but because of thoughtlessness and ignorance. It never crossed my mind to include her in activities that I now hunger for and drool over with my own sons and their families.

Now that I AM a mother-in-law (twice over) of married sons, I wish I had invited my husband's mother to take a much more active role in my life. If I could take a minute for a very long-distance phone call to Edna up in Heaven, I'd like to make a long overdue amend:

"Edna, I loved your quick sense of humor and your enormous heart. I now know how much you loved your son. I now know that you would have sold your soul to occupy a larger spot in his adult life. When you looked at Michael, I now know that you saw him at various ages. One smile from him could tap into a stored memory of him as a toddler. A certain facial expression could remind you of a time when he was bullied in elementary school. A lifetime of growth and development played in your mind with every visit you had with him -- just like it does for me now! You held all those treasures in your heart, just as I hold my sons' childhoods in mine. I deeply regret that I did not appreciate your mother-son bond. It truly never dawned on me. For that I am very sorry."

I know I'm not alone in my regret. My friends – other mothers of married sons – have also acknowledged their insensitivity toward their husbands' mothers. But for most of us, it's too late to turn it around.

The inspiration for this book came to me in a flash of brilliance! So many people have changed their lives by committing to various 12-Step programs. Each Step helps build a philosophy to create a more positive, productive, satisfying life. Stemming from many conversations with my M.O.M.S. friends (Mothers of Married Sons), I have crafted a special 12-Step program designed to help us integrate into our sons' lives with grace, dignity and love.

While certain 12-Step programs aren't meant for everyone, neither is this one meant for all mothers of married children. This is written from the heart for devoted mothers of married sons who want to graciously accept their new positions as mothers-in-law.

Just as I was very lucky to have had the perfect mother-in-law, I am also blessed to have two perfect daughters-in-law in Kristen and Lacey. They love their husbands, they have solid values and they are deeply committed to family. I adore each of them. My reactions to situations reflect MY insecurities and flaws – not theirs. I tend to lead with my emotions that often demand a great deal of Monday Morning Quarterback review and critique! I have broadened my outlook, accepting that there are many "right" ways to navigate through Life and that my ways are not necessarily the best ways! It is imperative that Kristen and Lacey understand that in one of my fantasies, I am the Queen of England and should thus be afforded royal deference. After all, would Kate Middleton ever overstep the wisdom, desires or expectations of The Queen?

Introduction

From the time I was a little girl, I had always dreamt of having children – lots of them. I mothered an entire family of dolls ranging from newborns all the way up to an almost life-sized five-year-old version of me. I dressed them, fed them, bathed them, walked them, read stories to them and even home schooled them. Yes – I did it all. I was a Super-Mom, practicing and honing my skills for the eventuality of my REAL family, and I absolutely loved every minute of it. (I wore invisible Wonder Woman bracelets and the glitter-and-star-studded cape! I was THAT good!)

Of course, Life seldom follows a drawn blueprint, modified, perfected and stored away for The Right Time, so my perfect world with a loving, devoted, faithful prince of a husband and a growing brood of children living in a house with a white picket fence, two cats, a bowl full of goldfish, perhaps a turtle or two and a dog never fell at my feet. Instead, I found myself at thirty years old, a single mother, raising two sons by myself. BOYS!! A two-year-old and a four-year old! BOYS! BY MYSELF! Did I mention they were boys?!

After ending my eight year marriage to an emotionally and physically abusive husband and serial philanderer, I assumed the enormous responsibility of parenting; of being both the mother

AND the father; nurturing, guiding, disciplining, teaching. Everything
. . . while at the same time conquering fears and insecurities that
perhaps I wasn't good enough – that I wasn't up to the task. I felt
enormously guilty (as Catholics are prone to do!) about failing at
marriage -- even though the situation was criminally abusive. How
could I teach my boys to hurl a football with that spiral spin when I,
myself, threw like a girl? Or, how could we discuss the strategies in a
baseball game when my favorite part was stretching my legs at the
hot dog stand during the seventh inning stretch? Who would counsel
them on all the "guy things?" Who would sit down with them to
explain the birds and the bees? Who would shape their characters,
provide for them -- physically, emotionally, morally, ethically? I
WOULD, that's who!

After seven years of single parenting, my sons and I blended
our little family when I married a wonderfully decent and moral
man. Despite the fact that my new husband, Michael, qualified for
the Most Wonderful Man for Me to Marry award, he was still a
stepfather. We bought books on the topic, discussed strategies on
how to build my sons' respect for him and operated like a family that
had not suffered a divorce. But we had. The boys travelled back and
forth to their father's house every other weekend, and for longer
periods of time over the summers and at holiday breaks. This was
just a fact of life that came with the territory.

Both Franklin D. Roosevelt and William Shakespeare's words echoed in my mind – on a daily basis. "The only thing to fear is fear itself," and "To thine own self be true" became my internal mantras. No pity party for me. There was simply no time! I faced my situation head on (not as gracefully or as courageously as hindsight tells me I should have, mind you) but a few clinks of my wrists, activating the powers of the invisible Wonder Woman bracelets transformed me into my super-hero alter ego.

My father and my brother stepped in and stepped up as male influences. They wrestled with my sons, included them in woodworking projects and helped them build model cars and airplanes. My brother took time from his own three sons to participate in Cub Scout and Indian Guide activities with them and even coached a couple of their baseball teams. "Bucky," (my boys' name for my father) supported them on the sidelines of T-ball games, soccer games, football games, school recitals, talent shows, science fairs – everything. They attended First Communion and Confirmation rites and Bucky even sponsored one of the boys in Confirmation. I am forever grateful to them both for loving my children and being an active presence in their early childhood experiences.

Timothy ("Tim") and Andrew ("Drew"), my babies, were my world – and for a long time, I was theirs. Whenever there was a school field trip, I made sure they had a little spending money in their pockets to buy a snack or a small memento of the day. Each time, however, Tim returned home with a gift for me! He used his money to buy ME a present! Those gifts -- but more importantly, the thoughts behind those gifts -- are more precious to me than anything money can ever buy. Oftentimes when Drew was at a friend's house on an after-school play date, he called home to check in with me. Invariably, just before saying "good-bye," he made sure to say, "I love you, Mom!" You can imagine the ribbing he got from his friends when this practice continued into middle school! Nevertheless, Drew continued to close all of his phone calls home with, "I love you, Mom!" Finally, after incessant teasing, Drew responded to his friends, "Hey! What's the matter with you guys? I love my mom! You got a problem with that?" And from then on, ALL of his friends ended their phone calls home with, "I love you, Mom!"

It's easy to understand just how strong my bond became with my two sons. I could not have been more proud of them. I admired the fact that they had grown into my two strong young men, interested in all the things guys like to do, but they also demonstrated such security with their identities that they weren't afraid to show their softer sides either. They were very well rounded and very self-assured. They had become the adult children of my dreams! They didn't get that way by following my fantasy blueprint. They got there by way of the "Plan B" that blindsided us from early on. I had raised two fine men. Mission: Accomplished!

Or so I thought! Patting myself on the back with an "Atta Girl!" and ready to ride off into the sunset into a "happily ever after" with a job well-done, I began envisioning the next phase of my relationship with my sons as they each found the woman of their dreams – their wives and my daughters-in-law. Hearts and flowers danced in the air. Songbirds serenaded and fluttered about. Ours was a scene from a fairy tale! All was well with the world! Tim, Drew and I would march through the future, together, with the same intensity of connectedness that we'd had for the past twenty-five years. We were the Three Musketeers with the "all for one and one for all mentality! Ahhhhhh . . . Life was Good!

And that's when it happened. I suddenly found myself in an entirely different role! I was no longer a mom – I am now a M.O.M.S. – a Mother of a Married Son.

I WILL say, from the get-go, that both of my daughters-in-law are the perfect mates for my sons. They each complement and complete their spouses. I could not have chosen better wives for my sons if I had been asked. I love them and respect them entirely. I will champion them and support them and encourage them --

always. I also offer this work for them. In time, they might become a Mother of a Married Son too, so . . . Girls -- we're in this together, for each other; my gift to you, as you have been to me. I love you.

The crisis is mine and mine alone. I am no longer the "prima ballerina" in my boys' eyes. After a lifetime of being Number One, I am reduced to lower case letters – mom. I am in the back seat, on the back burner, at the bottom of the in-box. I am the crumpled receipt forgotten at the bottom of the bag! What do I do with this serious demotion? Numerous internal arguments between my rational and emotional selves ensued:

"How can I be tossed aside like yesterday's News?" I whined.

"STOP IT!" admonished me as Super-Mom, "you've raised them to be strong, independent MEN! They're doing what they're supposed to be doing – taking a WIFE – making HER Number One!"

"But . . . they're MY boys!" continued the whimpering.

"Ahhhhhh . . .," admonished Super-Mom, "you didn't see this coming, did you? You're going to have to take a reality check and ADJUST!"

So "adjust" is just what I'm doing. I have chosen to find humor in my new status, and I strongly encourage others like me to follow suit. I am certain that there are other M.O.M.S. out there with similar, if not identical identity crises as mine. I am offering this 12-Step program for Mothers of Married Sons as a guidebook across the uncharted territory of our new roles as "the mother-in-law!"

M.O.M.S. Unite!!

The Serenity Prayer

God, grant me the

SERENITY

to accept the things

I cannot change

COURAGE

to change the

things I can

and

WISDOM

to know the difference

<u>M.O.M.S.</u>

<u>A 12-Step Guide for Mothers of Married Sons</u>

1. Admit that you are powerless over new female influences– that Life (and the status you once enjoyed as the most important woman in your son's life) has changed.

2. Come to believe that YOU are the one responsible for your happiness.

3. Keep your mouth shut. This will not be easy, but DO IT.

4. Come to understand that "What do you think?" IS NOT A QUESTION!

5. Share your insecurities and experiences with your friends. Ask for their support, feedback and understanding.

6. Forgive all family (and extended family) members who have innocently and unintentionally stepped on your feelings. Do NOT harbor ill will.

7. Flatter your daughter-in-law – and genuinely <u>mean</u> it.

8. Do not complain.

9. Never put your son in the middle – between you and your daughter-in-law and/or her family.

10. Do not be a doormat. Remember: It's O.K. to have feelings!

11. Personify and embody those words on the plaque: Be the Change You Want to See in the World (of mothers-in-law!) By doing so, the old stereotype of the mother-in-law as a beast will shatter! Young mothers of sons will be more aware of their future role!

12. Enjoy your new friendship with your daughter-in-law.

Step 1: Admit That You Are Powerless Over New Female Influences - that Life (and the status you once enjoyed as the most important woman in your son's life) is no more.

"Sure you're powerless, sure you're just one person, sure you can't change anything, but you don't have to be miserable about it as well."

- Lydia Lunch

Many 12-Step programs have adopted Albert Einstein's definition of *insanity*: repeating the same action over and over again and expecting a different outcome. And like these same 12-Step programs, M.O.M.S. also uses this definition.

For centuries, M.O.M.S. have commandeered many celebrations -- and in my case, for over a quarter of a century -- from birthday parties to end of season team awards banquets, cast parties, graduations, family dinners, and religious milestones -- just to name a few. We have planned, prepared, organized, orchestrated, followed through and executed these events successfully -- like professional event planners.

When our sons marry, however, we feel as if we've been stripped of all competence and ability -- not only in the eyes of our daughters-in-law and their mothers but also in the eyes of our sons. The reality may be quite different entirely, and most probably is, but . . . in our minds, we've been reduced to insignificant rubble. We tiptoed through the weddings, traversed through those first obstacle course holiday plans and adjusted to less frequent phone calls and personal visits from our sons. We pretend that we are "taking it in stride," but deep in our hearts we are grieving the loss of our positions as "#1 woman in our sons' lives." Everyone longs to be valued, but here we are, at the threshold of CHANGE! It is more difficult for a M.O.M.S. to transition from champion-level Capable Multitasker #1 Mom to Silent Bump on a Log than it is for a CEO of a Fortune 500 company to peacefully settle into retirement! Oh! The irony! We, like that successful chief executive officer, have worked hard for many years. We look forward to the point in our lives when we can relax and enjoy the fruits of our labor. So, why then, is it so difficult to really enjoy it when the time comes?

I had always heard that mothers of grooms were supposed to "wear beige and shut up!" but it was not until I WAS the mother of a groom that those words resonated with clarity! Being literal, I was under the misconception that "wearing beige" meant that my gown had to be a neutral color on my son's wedding day. I never imagined that "wearing beige" was really a metaphor for my new role and that "wearing beige" lasted far beyond that day. In fact, Mothers of

Married Sons really have to move into "The World of Beige!" Just as Alice fell through the rabbit hole into Wonderland, we M.O.M.S. also find ourselves in a new world but we KNOW we didn't fall through any hole! We're not quite sure how or when it happened, but . . . there are suddenly lots of strange things happening around us! Alice confronted new quirky characters, each throwing unforeseen situations in her direction. The Queen of Hearts, Tweedle-Dee and Tweedle-Dum, the Mad Hatter, the White Rabbit, the Cheshire Cat and many others also make cameo appearances in The World of Beige. Oh yes! They are all members of our own families, but we also become acquainted with others just like them -- through marriage! While our own families certainly have colorful characters, we've become accustomed to them and their oddities. "Oh! That's just Aunt Betty being . . . well, . . . Betty," we explain. But there is no booklet containing character sketches of your new daughter-in-law's family. We M.O.M.S. navigate through the minefield of introductions and small talk with great uncertainty and trepidation!

The most powerful new character in the World of Beige is not a person, but rather a relationship: the mother-daughter relationship between daughter-in-law and her mother. Las Vegas odds are against Superman, the Man of Steel, and his ability to crack that bond! In the mind of a M.O.M.S., that bond is set; it is magnificently powerful; it is solid; it is impenetrable. No amount of kryptonite can weaken it!

My first experience with The Bond That Never Breaks was during an Easter dinner. Loretta, Kristen's mother, included my husband and me in their family celebration just after Kristen and Tim became engaged. Michael and I were happy to attend. We were both very comfortable with family holiday dinners as both of our families also celebrated these events. My parents always invited my aunt and uncle, my brother and sister, their spouses and children and they often included our parish priests and others with no family of their own to visit. I was used to large feasts and family. It was customary for my sister-in-law, Andrea, and me to arrive early in the day to help with the preparations. We set the expansion leaves in the formal dining room table, and selected the fanciest table linens, fine china, crystal, sterling silver flatware and centerpieces. The "kids' table" was set, too, with whimsical Fitz & Floyd dinnerware and individual party favors pertinent to the holiday. My mother officiously planned the seating arrangements and placed the assignments, names printed in calligraphy and set into sterling silver place card holders, around the table (only to be stealthily rearranged by Andrea and me! (Far be it for either one of us to endure a holiday meal seated between two of our own family's versions of Tweedle-Dee or The Mad Hatter!)

Michael and I arrived at Loretta's house on Easter Sunday, eager to welcome (and to be welcomed by) Kristen's family. Loretta couldn't have been a more gracious hostess. She hugged and kissed each of us -- on both cheeks -- and escorted us through the house, introducing us to everyone there: her parents, her sister and brother-in-law, her nieces and nephews and their children, cousins, cousins of cousins, and cousins of cousins of cousins; SO MANY PEOPLE! Was it possible to have a family that large? If I didn't know better, I would have thought that I was in the church hall after the 11:00 a.m. Mass attending a parish-wide Easter feast! Yet, ALL of these people were members of Kristen's family!

The dining room table had been pushed to one side of the room in order to accommodate a more efficient buffet line. The women of the family busied themselves in the kitchen, preparing specialty dishes, chatting, laughing, assigning tasks to the younger girls and very obviously enjoying each other. Loretta, clearly the Master Chef/Event Planner, carefully studied her handwritten notes. She handed a few serving utensils to one of her nieces to place on the buffet table; Kristen dutifully followed Loretta's instructions to adjust some of the platters already on the table to make room for fresh flowers. All items on the list still not entirely checked off, further instructions were given to restock the outside coolers with soft drinks and beer and to fill the candy dishes with mints. The men congregated outdoors in the backyard attending to the traditional roasting of an entire whole pig! Loretta emerged from the house to supervise the progress on the pig. The mechanics of the family operated in rhythm -- like a well-oiled machine. Again I was struck at the genuine camaraderie that everyone shared. As a family that had emigrated from Italy to Argentina and then to the United States, they spoke in a mixture of Italian, Spanish and English. Fluency in spoken language was not necessary, however, to communicate the love and affection that was displayed by the entire group! I was edified and enchanted by this family and was absolutely thrilled to become a part of it! My son had chosen his bride well!

Loretta hustled and bustled about, clearly the omnipotent matriarch, putting the finishing touches on the celebration. She had arranged an Easter egg hunt for all of the cousins -- ages ranging from 2 to 12 years old! The older children were instructed to look for eggs hidden above their waists, leaving the obvious ones in the flowerbeds for the toddlers. Tim and Kristen's dogs had been confined to the garage. The teenagers and young adults of the family clustered together in the family room around the television, watching a baseball game and teasing each other unmercifully. Loretta had taken care of every detail!

When it was time to leave, Loretta made sure that everyone left with a package of carefully wrapped leftovers! I floated home on Cloud 9! What a fabulous family! Small vignettes of the day replayed in my mind, with Loretta being the central figure in each one. She had successfully orchestrated and executed the largest family gathering I had ever witnessed! Could it be that her Wonder Woman bracelets were more powerful than mine? Was her super-hero cape made of enchanted ermine and mine merely cheap common cotton? Was Kristen the 21st Century version of this domestic Titan? Were her skills just as finely honed as her mother's? Was I soon to be completely and entirely obliterated from a place of importance in my son's new world? Self-doubt came a-knocking at my door, but I was too enamored with the day to recognize it!

Weeks passed with Loretta and Kristen planning the wedding. They'd made to-do lists for everything: the engagement party, the church, the priest, possible reception sites, invitations, colors, flowers, bridal attendants, groomsmen, number of people to invite, crystal and china patterns, bridal showers, etc., etc., etc. Their world was a-flurry of everything bridal. Mother and daughter had joined forces; it was hard to tell where one left off and the other began! Loretta by herself is an amazing event planner, and she trained her daughter well! The two of them together are more powerful than the United Nations and NATO combined!

My insecurity grew with each planning event I attended. From the dress fittings to the cake tastings, I witnessed first-hand Kristen's flawless organizational skills and her extreme confidence! That girl KNEW what she wanted! She had the wedding dress designers offering to "take a tuck here," or " add a rosette there." Bakery chefs also bent to accommodate Kristen's original design ideas. How did she accomplish that with such charm and charisma? Was it her beauty? Her sweetness? Her creativity? Nope. It was her magic!

Kristen must have a particularly potent type of pixie dust in her pocket because she was able to get my son to do something that I couldn't EVER have done! One afternoon I received a phone call from Tim. Of course I'd asked about all the wedding plans, and that's all it took!

"You won't believe this! I literally have a list from A to Z itemizing everything I have to do before the wedding!" he said.

"Really? A list that long? What's on it?" I asked.

"Yes. REALLY," he stated emphatically, "Let's see here, . . . L, M, N, O, P . . . here's one, 'Prepare for Holy Communion!' What th' . . .? What's THAT supposed to mean? You just stand up, walk up the aisle of the church and get it!" he said.

Touched by Tim's obvious naïveté and amused at the notion of such a list, I offered, "Oh! I know what that means! You're supposed to go to Confession!"

"WHAT?!" he exploded, "No way!! I'm not doin' it! Got it?! NOT. DOIN'. IT!" he roared.

A few days passed before I received another call.

"Hey, Tim," I began, "so . . . how are you doing with The List? Are you making headway?"

"Yeah," he said, "I've ordered my tux, I've purchased gifts for the groomsmen and I've spoken with the Bishop about him marrying us."

"That's great! So . . . what about the 'Prepare for Communion' item? Did you go to Confession?" I asked, not knowing what kind of answer to expect.

"Uh . . . yes," he said more quietly than usual, "I went on Friday night!"

Wow! I was speechless! Here it was that I'd raised both of my sons as Roman Catholics but could never, EVER have gotten either one of them into church, much less Confession if my life depended on it! All Kristen had to do was put it on her To-Do List and . . . it happened!

Lesson learned that day: NEVER, NEVER, EVER MESS WITH POWER LIKE THAT!!!!

Step 2: Come to Believe that YOU are the One Responsible for Your Happiness

"People are just as happy as they make up their minds to be."

-- Abraham Lincoln

Happiness and the pursuit of it have long been the topics of intense research. It is an emotion determined by innate factors and perceptions as well as experiences. "Happiness," or "subjective well-being," according to psychologist Ed Diender, author of *Happiness: Unlocking the Mysteries of Psychological Wealth*, is defined as a combination of life satisfaction and having more positive than negative emotions. Martin Seligman, a leading researcher in positive psychology and author of *Authentic Happiness*, identifies three elements of happiness: (1) pleasure, (2) engagement and (3) meaning. He purports that it is this third element that is key in that people use their strengths to contribute to a larger purpose. Happiness has such great value that patriots such as Thomas Jefferson, Benjamin Franklin, John Adams and the entire Continental Congress included the phrase, " . . . life, liberty and the pursuit of happiness" in this country's Declaration of Independence!

Despite the notion that human beings have an inalienable right to be happy, the emotion can be as elusive as the pot of gold at the end of a rainbow! Oftentimes mood music lifts our spirits. Songs such as "Don't Worry, Be Happy" by Bobby McFerrin or Pharrell Williams' Grammy Award-winning "Happy" from the animated film, "Despicable Me 2," or Donovan's "Happiness Runs," just to name a few, can turn frowns upward, get the toes to tappin' and blow the clouds of gloom, doom and depression from the skies -- even if just for a while. But no matter how much background music is piped into our lives, no matter how many psychology books we read and no matter how many government philosophies we study, we are really only as happy as we decide to be!

M.O.M.S. must be particularly vigilant toward the pursuit of their happiness. M.O.M.S. must engage in rigorous self-study through the 12 steps to gracefully segue into this change of life. M.O.M.S. must make a conscious decision to BE HAPPY! In the early stages of a son's engagement, jubilation and rejoicing abound. There is so much activity, so much planning and so many parties, that even when "issues" DO develop, in most instances the gaiety continues and optimism prevails. M.O.M.S. witness the joy beaming from their sons that verifies that all is well with the world. However, it is good practice and strongly encouraged for new M.O.M.S. to begin attending meetings, making phone calls or emailing or video-chatting with friends or other M.O.M.S. for it is possible that those developing "issues" just may morph into the dreaded ferocious, green-eyed, fire-breathing beasts if not properly maintained. Why not be proactive rather than reactive? Chances are it's not the festering unresolved issues that are feeding the beasts but rather the sudden realization that the M.O.M.S. is missing her son, feeling lonely for what once was and being uncertain about what now is between her and her son.

Long after the wedding ceremony is over, the photo album tucked into a cupboard and time has passed, the lyrics from Paul Stookey's "The Wedding Song" should serve as a reminder to M.O.M.S. that "a man shall leave his mother and a woman leave her home, they will travel on to where the two shall be as one . . . And there is love!" It's natural. It's supposed to happen.

Then WHY is it so hard for some M.O.M.S. to be happy? It's simple. M.O.M.S. are bombarded with a tidal wave of emotional changes once their sons find that special someone. They just don't realize it! M.O.M.S. not only have to orient themselves to their new navigational coordinates on an ocean in a strange boat in uncharted waters, but they must also graciously defer to a younger woman who is the captain of her own ship in those same waters! Therein lies the challenge! A fully confident and capable mother of a son, comfortably directing her crew suddenly discovers that her crew has jumped ship and is sailing with a new captain. All at once, unless she wants to drift across the choppy sea alone, way out sight, she must turn her boat around and follow closely in the other's wake. It's all up to her and her alone!

I thought I had grown into my role as a mother of adult sons quite well after the younger of my two boys left for college. Tim had been the first to leave home to attend a university well over two hours from home. His progression into adulthood laid the foundation (or should have) for my adjustment into my changing mother role. He returned at holidays, but called on the phone less and less frequently and grew into his independence more rapidly than I expected. However, I understood that he was not my little boy anymore. He was a young man doing what young men are supposed to do. Tim DID come home from time to time and he DID initiate contact. I still felt important and valued. I was content. Drew, on the other hand, attended a service academy all the way on the other side of the country. I surrendered all parental authority to the United States Navy! Visits and telephone calls home were granted solely by the permission of a naval officer! Several Christmases passed without Drew's presence. The summer months did not find him returning home, hanging out with his high school friends or going to the beach. He belonged to the Navy. I felt lonely for Drew, but I was not unhappy. He called (when he could) and he e-mailed (again, when he was allowed). There was no crack, no break or no strain on our mother-son bond -- the U.S. Navy, and ultimately the United States Marines, were in there in a big way, but -- I understood. What REALLY threw me into a tailspin was the first time the Marines deployed Drew overseas. He had not yet become engaged, but the writing was on the wall -- in invisible ink. What the United States Marine Corps could NOT do to make me feel insecure about my relationship with my son, one very sweet, attractive, one hundred pound girl named Lacey could!

Prior to his departure to Okinawa, Japan, Drew was required to submit signed legal documents regarding his personal assets to be kept on file as part of the procedures consistent with military policies. My name was listed as beneficiary, next of kin, and as the first contact person in the event notification became necessary. I was privy to many details regarding his six-month stationing and was even given a photocopy of his official orders. I would have expected nothing less; I, of course, was his mother -- the most important person in Drew's life.

Michael and I hosted a small farewell dinner the weekend before Drew's scheduled departure. Invited guests included Lacey, her parents, and Joan and Tom (Michael's sister and brother-in-law who had been close friends with Lacey's family for years). During the course of the evening, I suggested to Lacey and Joan that we keep

30

Drew entertained and reduce any possible bouts of homesickness by staging monthly thematic vignettes, taking photos and writing creative stories to accompany them, then send them off in care packages containing candy and other special treats. They jumped at the idea! What a great director I was!

Our first photo shoot depicted a formal Japanese Tea Ceremony. The three of us dressed in matching red silk kimonos and drew heavy lines around our eyes to make us look as Japanese as possible. The Mikado's "Three Little Maids From School" had nothing on us! Tom snapped photos of us sipping tea, gazing out over the valley dramatically lost in thoughts of Drew, and standing beneath a cherry tree in full bloom. Lacey posed for single photos with a tear falling from the corner of each eye. We even tied a black belt that had come with the kimono costumes around its head and snapped a few pictures of him! Max is Drew's blonde Cairn Terrier/Poodle mix dog that Drew adopted during flight school. Pleased with the collection of photographs, we concluded the session brainstorming about the narrative that was to accompany them. Lacey volunteered to write the story, finish filling the care package and send it on its way.

Two weeks passed with me having forgotten about the care package. I answered the ringing phone.

"Hey Mom!" said Drew long distance from Japan.

"DREW!" I squealed with delight. "Oh my gosh! How ARE you? How was the flight over there? What are your accommodations like? Tell me EVERYTHING! Oh! Did you get our care package?" I asked, rambling a hundred miles a minute.

"Ha Ha! Yes. It was really funny! Lacey looks AWESOME in the pictures, doesn't she? And Max! What a little Ninja! I really miss that little guy!" he said, completely ignoring any mention of me or my involvement.

"Uh . . . ya, . . . Lacey looks cute, I guess," I said flatly. I absolutely refused to comment on the dog. If Drew couldn't mention ME, I certainly was NOT going to mention his DOG! The conversation continued and as I relayed current information about recent activity in our area, Drew told me that he already knew what I was telling him because LACEY had told him!

WAIT!!! WHAT???!!! When had he spoken with HER???!!!

"Oh . . . so . . . you already know all this," I said somewhat cautiously. "When did you talk to Lacey?"

"I talk to her every day!" he volunteered cheerfully.

WHAT???!!! WAIT --- EVERY DAY????? EVERY DAY???!!! EVERY BLESSED DAY???!!!

"Oh. You talk to Lacey every day? How's that? She works. When do you talk to her? There's what -- a nine hour time difference between here and Japan?!" I queried, trying not to sound jealous.

"She told me I could call her even if it's the middle of the night her time! She keeps her phone by her side when she goes to bed!" he explained.

Oh, BROTHER!!!!!!! What in the world is happening here??? He talks to her EVERY DAY?????!!!!! She sleeps with her PHONE???!!!

I could have been blown over by a feather! The impact of realizing that my status was in free fall hit me like a steamroller! My legs were no longer trusted supports for the weight that just been dropped onto my shoulders. I slumped onto the nearest chair, holding the phone to my ear, listening as Drew filled me in on his new experiences. Saying as little as possible in an effort not to betray the quiver in my voice, I bid my good-byes, told my son I loved him, hung up the phone and wept.

Not long after this disastrous day, my email inbox chimed receipt of a new message. Lacey wanted to know when the "Three

Little Maids" were going to stage Photo Shoot #2 for Care Package #2. Joan immediately responded, offering her house and backyard as the venue. I shook off my depression and dove right into preparations for the next theme. Since the year was in its final quarter and since Drew loves sports, football and tailgate parties were chosen as the theme. Again, several action shots of the three of us playing football dressed in football jerseys (rolled up hand towels stuffed inside as shoulder pads), grease paint under our eyes, a beer in one hand and a football in another collected on Tom's iPhone. While shopping for all of the props for this vignette, I happened upon a Halloween costume for Max -- a football! We dressed the poor dog and Tom snapped pictures of Lacey pretending to hurl him through the air on a Hail Mary pass! Care Package #2 was packed and posted!

I stayed at Joan's house long after Lacey left. We talked about how much fun it was to get together for these silly photo shoots and how much Drew enjoyed getting them. I told Joan about my phone call with Drew, how he already knew everything I had to tell him, how he spoke with Lacey EVERY DAY, and how I had been dethroned and discarded. She broke into hysterics.

"You are SO funny!" she laughed. "Drew's in love! With LACEY! That doesn't mean you've been 'dethroned and discarded, you Silly!'"

Maybe it was the beer we'd finished drinking or maybe it was the fact that I liked Lacey, but . . . I burst into laughter too. The more I described my devastation during the last phone conversation with Drew, the harder we howled with laughter!

"Ya," I said, " . . . and then I slunk into the chair and had ALL I could do to keep from sobbing so Drew wouldn't hear me!" I laughed.

"You are a crazy, crazy lady!" Joan said as she put her arms around me and gave me a big hug and a kiss right on the cheek.

Finally it was time for Drew's return home! Even though his scheduled arrival time was set for the wee hours of the morning, I planned to be present when the military caravan pulled into Camp Pendleton from March Air Force Base. I brought hand-painted and decorated posters which read, "Welcome Home, Drew!" and "We <heart> Drew!" on them to wave as he got off the bus. The "welcoming committee," Tom, Joan, me, Lacey and Max the dog stood shivering under the dark blanket of night for an eternity, waiting and waiting and waiting for the military convoy.

"There they are!" someone from another welcoming committee exclaimed. "They're coming over the hill!"

A crowd of excited family members and friends gathered together. Everyone, it seemed, had brought signs, flowers and pompoms to celebrate their loved ones' return! One by one, Marines exited the bus, smiling and rushing to their families. Just as we wondered if Drew had missed the first bus, his tall, athletic frame emerged from the vehicle. He looked as if he'd just awakened, blinking slowly at the brightness of the floodlights on the pavement. Slowly his mouth broadened into a full ear-to-ear grin and he leapt down the two stairs from the bus exit and toward us! I jumped up and down, happily waving my signs, not minding the cold temperature or the late hour! This was certainly worth every minute of the wait! Drew approached . . . nearer and nearer, but . . . he passed right by me and scooped Lacey up into his arms and held her close to him for a long, long time! When he finally let go of her, he reached for his dog, Max!!

It became fairly obvious that the only "welcoming committee" Drew was interested in had already been greeted! Tom and Joan joined in the merriment by wrapping their arms around Drew, Lacey and Max, creating a big group hug. My emotions alternated between joy and devastation! Of course I was thrilled that Drew had returned home after six months. Of course he looked healthy and happy. I even conceded that, if everything Joan had told me were true -- that Drew was in love with Lacey -- then of course he missed her and was anxious to be reunited with her. The six little words strung together as a question when Drew FINALLY noticed that I was there were uttered with his complete and genuine surprise: "Oh! Hey, Mom!! What are YOU doing here?"

Stunned into complete silence and not knowing whether to cry, scream or sob uncontrollably, I looked blankly at Joan! The expression on my face asked, "What just happened?" but when our eyes met, we both broke into uncontrollable laughter! I DID eventually get the warm greeting I'd been waiting for; I just didn't get it in the order or with the ecstatic enthusiasm I'd expected or wanted! During my drive home from the Marine Base, I reflected back on the evening. My son was home, he was safe, and he was in love. What more could a mother ask for?

Happiness is a choice. While I initially resented not being the Chief Information Officer in Drew's life -- both receiving and dispensing new and pertinent local and family scoops, I consciously focused on the bigger picture -- being happy. With Joan's broader perspective (and with her urging and encouragement) I was able to see how inappropriate it was for me to keep my claws tightly clutched onto my son. Soon I was able to find humor in my attitude! I literally let go of that "stinkin' thinkin'!"

Turn up the music! Replay "The Wedding Song" and sing along, especially the part of the verse that says, "a man shall leave his mother . . . and there is Love!" After that, do yourself a favor! Find an old Walkman or access the iTunes Store and download the theme song from the '70's TV sitcom, The Partridge Family -- "Come On! Get Happy!"

Step 3: Keep Your Mouth Shut

"If you can't say something nice, don't say anything at all!"

--- Thumper (to Bambi)

Ah! The wisdom of little Thumper's words rings so true, especially for M.O.M.S.! We remember passing along that same advice to our children throughout the years, and now it's time for us to apply it to our own lives. Before either one of my sons married, I listened to my friends relay vignettes about their married sons and how powerless they felt, knowing that they could restore peace and harmony in any given situation, except, no one ever asked! Sons don't seek help! After all, they're MEN! Everyone knows that men don't ask for directions when they're lost on the roads, so why should we expect them to seek help when they're lost on the domestic front? How can THAT be?! Strong support for Step 3: Keep Your Mouth Shut came to me from a good friend long before the 12-Step Program of M.O.M.S. had been conceived.

"I spend a lot of time biting my tongue!" she said, "You'll find that out too when you enter The World of Married Children!"

And how right she was! Many times during my transition into what I have named "The World of Beige," my friend's wise advice echoed in my mind. I bit my tongue so often that I even thought about learning American Sign Language in the event I ended up biting it off!

There were many instances where I practiced Step 3, but one of the most difficult times for deep tongue-biting came when my first grandchild was learning to talk. Everyone understands that all first-time parents are anxious to hear their child utter the two most precious and endearing words in the world, "Mama" and "Daddy," but their excitement and anticipation sorely pales in comparison to a grandmother's desire to hear that child utter the name by which she will be known! In my case, that name is "GiGi," (for Gorgeous Grandma! I believe that grandma names should be just as descriptive as they are easy to pronounce!)

Ever since my son, Tim, proposed to Kristen, (well, to be absolutely truthful, . . . ever since he started dating, I began tossing around several different names that could possibly become MY grandma name: Grandma, Granny, Grammie, Maw-Maw, Nana, and even Dodie (which is what my nephews call me). I surveyed my already-grandmothered friends and dismissed their names: YaYa, Dibby, Amah, Omah and Big Mom (good grief!)

For months, my sweet grandson, Parker, demonstrated that he KNEW who I was, by pointing to me whenever anyone asked,

"Where's GiGi?" and even bringing books and toys to me when so instructed, so I KNEW he KNEW me. BUT . . . there was no other validation as powerful as that of hearing him say my name.

The Marine Corps assigned my younger son, Drew, to the Kaneohe Marine Base on Oahu for three years, so when Parker was 18-months-old, Michael and I took Tim, Kristen and Parker there for a one-week visit at Christmas time. I was in absolute heaven! It didn't matter to me that we were in the beautiful, warm, lush, tropical islands. I could have been snowbound in the icy, biting Arctic tundra -- anywhere -- as long as my boys and their families were with me – alone – without any other family members! No in-laws. No ex-husband. No cousins. Nobody. But. ME. I selfishly indulged in all that alone time. I got to watch my sons be brothers -- teasing, boxing, wrestling, puffing themselves up, but most of all, just watching them display the deep love they have for each other. I also got to watch Kristen and Lacey get to know each other better. They chatted about fashions, yoga, hairstyles, cosmetics and hiking. They joked about their husbands, they planned and prepared our meals and they coordinated centerpieces with various table linens. They genuinely LIKED each other. They became the sisters that neither one ever had. And . . . I got to be with my Parker without having to compete with the other grandma for quality time. He was ALL MINE! I thought to myself, "Ah . . . this is SUCH a great family!"

Throughout the week, Parker's language developed. His unintelligible one-syllable utterances expanded into longer, four- and five-syllable unintelligible utterances --- sentences! He was just teetering on the edge of breaking through to real words! We all coaxed and prodded, encouraged and even begged him to speak, but . . . alas! The only words he said were "Ma" and "Da!" Progress, yes. Fireworks and call for celebration? Hardly!

Three weeks into the New Year, my cell phone buzzed to announce a new message. It was a video clip from Kristen! I clicked on it and watched as I heard her say, "Parker, can you say 'Mommy?'"

"Mommy!" he said as clear as a bell!

Could THIS be it? Is she showing me that he can finally say "GiGi?" Oh! Be still my heart! Ready the cannons!

"Parker! Can you say "Daddy?"

"Dad-DY!" he said.

"Parker! Parker – can you say "Nona?" (the name for the OTHER grandma, Kristen's mom!)

"No-na!" he repeated.

Oh . . . I'm next, I just know it . . . I can FEEL it . . .!!!

"Can you say "No-No?" came the next instruction.

"No-!" he said.

"Parker! What does a cow say?" she inquired.

Wait!! What? Did I miss it? What the heck? "WHAT DOES A COW SAY?" WHAT? A cow? Really?! A COW?

"Mooooo," he answered proudly.

OK. Relax! It's coming. Just be patient!

"Parker! What does a kitty say?" was the next question.

"Mew," he responded correctly.

"Parker! Can you say 'Chester?'" (the name of one of their dogs!)

OK – good! We're back to identifying things (at least!)

"Ches-," he said.

"Yea! Good boy! Can you say 'Mandy?'" (the name of their other dog!)

"Mannie-," he replied.

Ches -, Mannie- "Big deal!

"Good Boy!! Parker! What does a dinosaur say?" she asked.

"Raaaaaaaaaaaaahhhhhhhhh!" he roared.

Hmmmmm . . . cute, but what about, "Parker! Can you say, "GiGi?"

What does a pig say?" she inquired.

WHAT!!!???? Did I miss it again? A PIG? Seriously???? I don't even rate honorable mention before a pig? Is this really happening?!

"Oink!" he said proudly.

And with that, the clip ended.

I immediately replayed the video, thinking that I'd just missed hearing MY name. Nope. Didn't hear it. I listened again and again and again, hoping against hope that the audio on the clip had skipped or there had been a problem with the video-feed, but . . . after at least thirty tries, I faced the fact that I was below a pig! I did not rate, but a PIG did!!

OK. Dilemma: Do I say something to my daughter-in-law about the omission of my name in the video, thereby throwing a dagger into the relationship, or do I ignore the hurtful omission and stuff my feelings? Should I be happy that I was thought of in the first place and that I should feel grateful that I was even sent the video? A mere morsel of communication for the proverbial difficult *mother-in-law!?*

There are several ways I could have responded, but luckily, my thinking, rational brain won out. I literally launched a full-scale war with my emotional brain, forcing my fingers to type a text response of, "Wow!!! He knows SOOOOOOO many words!" and ended the text with a Smiley :). (My emotional brain had an entirely different message in mind!) After pressing SEND, I tossed the phone onto the table with more force than I had intended and sank into a dark pond of self-pity. (At least I was being a good mother-in-law and using Step 3 -- Keep Your Mouth Shut!)

A few days later, I sent a text message to Tim, confirming that I was still on schedule to babysit the following Monday. Instead of receiving a response from him, my cell phone sang its incoming call tone! Kristen's name appeared on the screen! She verified that I was indeed still expected. I commented about Parker's expanding vocabulary, and asked if he could say, "GiGi." I knew he was near her because I could hear him babbling in the background. She asked him, "Parker, can you say, 'GiGi?'" but he clammed up, not willing to perform. Once again, I became the victim of "delayed gratification!" I just was NOT going to hear my name!

Later that evening, my cell phone buzzed again to announce an incoming video clip. Afraid to watch it, lest it be just another demonstration of many words Parker had in his expanding vocabulary EXCEPT GiGi, I left my phone on the table. However, it was as if the phone itself sent magnetic forces to pull me toward it. I couldn't leave it there with that video clip left unwatched! I gingerly picked up the phone and cautiously clicked on the video icon.

"Parker! Can you say "GiGi?" came Kristen's voice.

"GiGi!" said Parker as clear as a bell!

"Good Boy!! Parker, can you say GiGi again?" she prodded.

"GiGi!" he said -- again!

I was literally over the moon with joy! I AM ON THE MAP!!! YES!!!!!

My response text?

"OMG! Thank you! That made my day! :)" (Gotta love those Smileys!)

Step 4: Come to Understand that "What Do You Think?" IS NOT A QUESTION!

"Every step of life shows much caution is required."

--Johann Wolfgang von Goethe

"Communication" as defined by the online World Dictionary is the imparting or interchange of thoughts, opinions or information by speech, writing or signs. Early Man conveyed meaning to one another by using grunts, crying out or making other sounds. For a period of over 100,000 years, Man continued to refine these grunts and sounds into more specific tones and syllables that gradually developed into spoken language. Gestures and facial expressions often accompanied the spoken words to emphasize or clarify meaning. Tribes migrated into distant and disparate regions, causing variations in the language. Each group continued to communicate in its own way, with each particular language changing and developing into its own independent method of communicating. Populations grew, languages changed and splinters or dialects of very similar languages emerged. Modern linguists cannot even pinpoint the exact number of languages that exist across the globe today!

Fluency in foreign languages is becoming more and more valuable. International travel has increased, world politics has become more complicated and the need for multi-national collaboration has become crucial to the health of this planet. Educators have even designed many children's programs around multilingual curricula to facilitate the push toward bilingualism. International students leave their parents and families as early as middle school to reside in other countries for the express purpose of becoming fluent in another language. Great emphasis has been placed on language and even greater steps have been taken to focus on all aspects of learning language: its idioms, figures of speech, voice tones, inflections, formal speech, casual speech and body language. It takes years for a student to become as fluent as a native speaker -- years.

M.O.M.S., in addition to being confronted with a mountain of emotional transitions, are also required to take a crash course in a foreign language. There are no textbooks for this one; no tapes, no Rosetta Stone computer programs, no podcasts, no CDs, no adult education classes, nothing! This particular foreign language doesn't even have a name! M.O.M.S. are thrown into a total immersion course in the emotional language that has grown between her son and his wife. M.O.M.S. understand the spoken word, that's for certain! But it is the shades of meaning, the body language and the facial expressions that cloud the meanings of those words!

Having taught English as a Second Language for over thirteen years, I should have picked up on certain cues indicative of a language barrier. One Taiwanese student, returning after summer break, rushed to greet me, saying, "Oh! Mrs. West! You look like trunk of tree!" I knew what a trunk of a tree looked like, and I also read her facial expression correctly. She was happy to see me and she thought she was giving me a compliment. I knew there had been a communication breakdown somewhere -- I just wasn't sure where! During the morning break in the faculty lounge, I asked my colleagues if it looked as if I'd gained weight over the summer. I explained my reason for the question. Later in the day, another teacher mentioned to this student that she had hurt my feelings by telling me that I resembled the trunk of a tree. Antonia was mortified! She meant to tell me that I looked like a TWIG of a tree rather than the trunk! I knew then that I had to revise my lesson plans for the week (or month or however long it took) to focus intently on idioms! If only it were that easy to modify the lesson plans for M.O.M.S.!

Lesson One in the unnamed foreign language is: The sentence, "What do you think?" is NOT a question. That string of words complies with all of the grammatical criteria of a question in the English language, but beware. It begins with an interrogative, the subject and verb order are inverted and the ending punctuation is a question mark, but still . . . it is NOT a question.

My first exposure to Lesson One came during the months of Tim and Kristen's engagement. I was a neophyte in M.O.M.S. -- a Level One Beginner. I had yet to realize that my identity was in flux and that Life had enrolled me in a new foreign language without a name. Joy, excitement and wedding plans covered those challenges like a beautiful freshly fallen blanket of lily-white snow. I danced on top with delight, completely unaware of the dangers beneath.

"Mom -- we're going to have an engagement party at Gladstone's! What do you think?" Tim asked. "We're inviting about forty-five people for a cocktail reception and a steak and lobster dinner!"

"Just tell me when and what time, and we'll be there!" I answered, matching the excitement in Tim's question. My gut whispered that such a party seemed a bit extravagant, but I paid it no heed.

The planning continued with everything moving forward gliding atop the glistening white blanket of snow. I attended wedding cake tastings where the string of words, "What do you think?" followed each bite.

"It's delicious!" were my honest responses.

Dress fittings, invitation samples, bridal registry choices -- from everyday flatware to sterling silver serving pieces to china patterns and crystal -- all evoked that string of words, "What do you think?"

"I like 'em all!" I continued to answer with genuine honesty, still not comprehending Lesson One.

Two wedding showers under my belt with me still using, "I like EVERYTHING!" as a response, Level One, Lesson One remained unmastered. I had never varied my response. It was during the wedding reception dinner tasting at the Bel-Air Bay Club that I made a mental note to study the previous pages of my new language program more thoroughly. Four different dinner salads sat on the table in front of us. Tim, Kristen, Loretta (Kristen's mother) and I sampled each one.

"What do you think?" Kristen posed to all of us.

"I like 'em all!" I responded in my usual way. I really DID like them all, and I felt that any of the four would have been lovely choices for the reception. What did it matter anyway? It was just a salad!

"Uh . . . I'm not sure about the beefsteak tomato in this one," critiqued Loretta. "It's August now, but I don't think they're going to be good in December!" Mother and daughter exchanged glances and the corners of their mouths contorted into shapes that conveyed displeasure -- not quite frowns, but definitely not smiles.

Whoa!! I'm SO out of my league here! I hadn't even noticed the type of tomato!

"I don't think it really matters," I said, "Nobody's going to care if beefsteaks aren't available! I'm sure they'll be substituted with another type that will be just as good! Gosh! People probably won't even notice if there are tomatoes in the salad or not!"

There. I'd offered input -- for the first time! I ventured into oral practice following Lesson One.

"Substitute another type of tomato?? What kind? We have to be sure or the whole salad's personality will be different!" Kristen and Loretta both agreed.

<GASP!> *Uh oh. You'd better not talk! You're not ready yet! Study some more! Go back to Page 1 of Lesson One: "What do you think? is NOT a question. Could that really be true? Noooooooo!*

We finished the complimentary tasting with me truly enjoying every delicious mouthful. I remained quiet, just listening to all of the comments about each dinner course, as I mentally drilled the vocabulary exercises of Lesson One. Tim also seemed quiet, but when Kristen pressed for a decision, he ultimately chose his preference, ending any indecision. Sometimes he didn't have to speak at all! Just a tilt of his head in one direction or a certain sigh was all that was needed to convey his meaning.

The wedding long past, I was back at home and growing increasingly confused about many things about myself, my changing identity and my brand new role as a mother-in-law. I naively denied that I had been immersed in learning a new language and that I had yet to pass the test on Lesson One! I was concentrating on being a really good, agreeable mother-in-law! I refrained from calling too often, sending e-mails or forwarding cute videos to the newly-married couple in an effort to give them their space. "Gladys Kravitz" was NOT who I was!

It wasn't too long before my other son popped the question to Lacey that I had more opportunities to practice Lesson One. This time, however, the lesson seemed invalid!

Drew's wedding was planned and executed in rapid speed progression! From the actual proposal right through to the wedding date, everything ran in Fast Forward. Since Drew had attended the United States Naval Academy, I had assumed that he would marry in the chapel on The Yard, in full dress blues. After the nuptials, he and his bride would exit the chapel beneath a tunnel of crossed swords. It was one of my dreams that I knew wouldn't come true. However, when Drew called to fill me in on the whirlwind plans, I heard him ask me, "What do you think?"

Aaauuughhh!!! "What do you think?" There it is again!
Review: Lesson One -- "What do you think?" is NOT a question. Is it really true?

"Mom. I've invited my entire squadron to the wedding, and since the wedding is in mid-September, it's probably going to be really hot, so . . . I'm just going to wear khakis and a Hawaiian shirt instead of my dress uniform. What do you think?"

"WHAT DO I THINK???!!! WHAT DO I THINK!!!??? WHAT DO YOU THINK I THINK!!!??? Drew!!! This is your WEDDING!!! It's one of the most important days of your life! You're actually serious about wearing khakis and a Hawaiian shirt ---- like it's no big deal? Like you're going to a pig roast or something?" I wailed.

"Well . . . here's the deal with having members of the military at the wedding. If I, as the groom, wear my dress blues, everybody in my squadron has to wear theirs. If I choose to be more casual, then they don't have to dress up. They can be casual too! Some of the guys don't want to get dressed up!" he explained.

"Oh! Well, then . . . ." I began, sarcasm dripping from every syllable, "by ALL means, let's make sure the boys are comfy, shall we? We wouldn't want them to break out in a sweat now, would we? Poor babies!"

"It's probably going to be over 80 degrees!" Drew offered.

"So WHAT?! Jeezuz criminy, Drew!!! This is YOUR WEDDING! You are supposed to respect the rite of matrimony -- not treat it like a Saturday afternoon luau! If your friends don't want to wear their uniforms, then they don't have to come to the wedding!" I insisted. "You asked me what I think, so . . . I told you! If you didn't want my opinion, then you shouldn't have asked for it!"

"O.K., calm down already!" he said, "I'll wear the uniform!"

So . . . "What do you think?" really IS a question??? I don't get it.

I totally empathized with my ESL students when they shook their heads and said, "Aahhh! I so confuse!"

Which was it? Was "What do you think?" a question or was it NOT? More opportunities for discovery and learning presented themselves! Upon learning that Tim and Kristen were expecting a baby, there was great call for celebration. Loretta called and asked if I would participate in planning a baby shower. I was delighted beyond words to be included, especially since my feelings of worth had taken a nosedive. M.O.M.S., or at least THIS one, felt no sense of purpose in her family anymore. Typical empty nest syndrome? Perhaps. Nevertheless, I had been specifically drawn into planning an event for my daughter-in-law! This was a chance to show that I still mattered!

Level One, Lesson One should also include a definitions section. "Baby shower" should be among them. My understanding of the term meant: a small to mid-sized gathering of women coming together over a light meal and perhaps a game or two to celebrate the upcoming birth of a baby of a family member or close friend. Baby showers that I'd attended had been held at someone's home. A buffet luncheon of chicken salad -- or something along those lines -- croissants, a fruit platter and a cake was set out on the dining room table while gifts were collected on the coffee table in the living room. Streamers, balloons and stuffed animals and baby toys decorated the rooms. Level One, Lesson One should also include a section on culture(s) and possible pitfalls and culture clash. These two sections would be of extreme value to the Level One Beginner!

Kristen comes from an extremely close, large Italian family. I do not. Every event for Kristen's family is a cause of gaiety and celebration on a grand scale. I truly envy their close bond. However, my participation on the planning committee for Kristen's baby shower was as disastrous as asking a first grade room mother to plan the Inaugural Ball for the President of the United States! I was untrained, unprepared and unqualified!

A phone call from Loretta, early in the planning stages, indicated just how over my head I was.

"Hi, Peggy! I've just gone to The Ayres Hotel to reserve one of their smaller banquet rooms for the shower. They gave me a couple of their sample menus so we can see what they have to offer and how they can switch some things out. I'll fax them to you, but I think the breast of chicken with risotto and arugula looked nice. That's $25.99 per person plus tax and tip. Oh! And there's a children's menu for $15.99 per person plus plus! What do you think? Then there's champagne and a fruit punch. I didn't cost that out yet, but the corkage fee is $12.00 per bottle.

"I also checked with their florist. She can make up centerpieces -- really cute ones -- for $39.99 a piece. I told her I liked the little baskets with fresh spring flowers in them. I also picked out a darling grosgrain ribbon that can be intertwined in the baskets. SO cute! I figured we'll need about eight of those. Do you like that idea? What do you think?

"Then there's the cake! The Ayres Hotel can provide a cake, but I'd like to go with a really nice bakery that I know of. Their cakes are to die for! I think a whole sheet cake will be enough, but just in case, I also think we should get a cupcake tree -- for the little ones, you know?! What do you think?"

What do I think????? You don't want to know what I think!!!!

"Uh . . . how many people are we inviting?" I asked, my voice trembling in fear.

"About sixty," replied Loretta.

Math is definitely not my strong suit, but very quickly off the top of my head, I rounded the cost of the chicken/risotto/arugula to $35.00 per person and multiplied that by 60 -- $2,100 just for the food! I was completely overwhelmed! For that same amount of money, I could have planned at least six baby showers -- according to MY definition of terms!

Now I REALLY had a dilemma on my hands: I was so happy to prove that I still had value in the family and I was thrilled to have been included, BUT I had no experience with this level of baby shower before and felt that it was a bit extravagant, to say the least! Should I continue to give my standard response of "I love everything!" or should I answer the question, "What do you think?" honestly?

"Yikes, Loretta!! That all sounds amazing, but . . . wow! It's so fancy for a baby shower! I hate to say it, but . . . it so expensive!" I said with more apprehension in my voice than I'd intended.

I hated myself the minute the words escaped from my mouth, but there was no pulling them back in. Plop a cone-shaped hat on my head and drape a sandwich sign over my shoulders that reads "Party Pooper" on it! I felt worse about my role in the family now than had I not been asked to participate at all! But . . . I'd opened my mouth, so it was time for some major damage control.

"I don't mean to be such a damper on the festivities, but my idea of a baby shower is a lot lower key than this! I'd offer to have it at my house, but I live so far away!" I suggested delicately.

"I'd have it here, but the backyard isn't planted with flowers and I don't want to have to worry about weather," Loretta explained.

"I understand, and I get that," I said, "but . . . don't you think it's a lot of money to spend on a shower? Maybe we could go together on a crib and dresser for them or something."

"But . . . this is just our way!" Loretta explained.

I knew then that she was right -- it was "their way." Kristen had grown up with celebrations like this and there was no place for my input. This is the type of shower that she expected and looked forward to ever since she dreamed of having a baby.   My opinions simply didn't belong.

Another study session with the unwritten textbook on the language without a name revealed a further clarification of one of the language's nuances:

Level One, Lesson One: "What do you think?" is NOT a question, but rather an invitation to give assent to whatever is being suggested. If, however, "What do you think?" is spoken from the son of a M.OM.S., then it is indeed a question.

While I still do not have the fluency of a native speaker of the language without a name, I am superbly functionally fluent. Whenever I hear the words, "What do you think?" from ANYONE, alarm bells blast through my head!

Aaaaauuuugggggghhhh!!!! There's that string of words again! It's a trap!!! Remember: make SURE it's a question!!!

After shutting off the siren's warning of potential danger, I always respond with, "Do you really want to know what I think or are you merely thinking out loud?"

Level One, Lesson Two: Every step of life shows that much caution is required.

Step 5: Share Your Insecurities and Experiences with Your Friends. Ask for Their Support, Feedback and Understanding

"Surround yourself with people who provide you with support and love and remember to give back as much as you can in return."

--Karen Kain

People committed to working 12-Step programs garner support and encouragement from each other. They regularly attend meetings; they network through each other over the telephone or at smaller, more intimate gatherings; they read literature written especially for their issues; they even ask someone within the program whom they admire to be their sponsor for extra, individual support. M.O.M.S. is so new, and in its infancy, has not as yet reached the masses, but those who DO know of it are wildly enthusiastic to participate in much the same way as its predecessor 12-Step participants. In fact, the whole idea for M.O.M.S. came to me in the midst of a small gathering of people in my community who informally meet in a beautiful park in the late afternoon every day for one hour while their dogs romp and play. We affectionately dubbed the hour "Doggie Club." The conversations usually revolve around newly released movies, local politics, upcoming vacation plans, golf or recent vacation recaps. There are no earth-shattering, in-depth discussions. Just light banter.

My older son had recently become engaged and I was just beginning to realize how my position was changing. I had not yet given birth to M.O.M.S., so I resisted this transition with the vehemence of a venomous viper! I arrived at the park every day with a new episode over which to rant and rave! The older, more seasoned people in the group reacted with laughter! They had endured similar experiences when their sons married! I heard story upon story upon story of wedding plans gone awry, in-laws becoming outlaws, friends becoming enemies, brothers and sisters disowning each other and brides breaking off the engagements, etc. Nearly everyone in the group had a story to tell; and the reaction from the rest of us was not anger, but rather empathy, and encouragement, then ultimately humor. At the end of the hour, we all re-leashed our dogs and left the park feeling . . . happy! I found myself actually looking forward to the next day's meeting -- not to exercise and socialize my dog! No!!! I couldn't wait to feel the warm support from that small group of people.

A little while later, I happened to be in the grocery store checkout line with a very good friend of mine named Renee. We were discussing some of my son's engagement scenarios and my growing feelings of being cast aside, when I jokingly blurted out,

"You know what?! I should create a 12-Step program for mothers of married sons! I'll bet you there are a lot of women out there just like me who are feeling the way I do!"

Unbeknownst to me, the customer behind us had been eavesdropping! She must have liked what she heard, because she softly interrupted us, saying,

"Excuse me, but I really wish you would! I'd even volunteer to become a charter member! My son is married and boy! Do I ever need someone to talk to!"

All three of us laughed at the notion of being a "charter member" of my fictitious group! My groceries all bagged and loaded into the cart, Renee and I continued out to the car. Even though I'd said it out loud -- that "I should craft a 12-Step program for mothers of married sons" -- I was still only half serious! I liked the idea well enough, absolutely! But I hadn't committed to actually DOING it! Days and weeks passed with me gaining emotional strength from the members of Doggie Club. I felt stronger and more self-assured. I kept tossing the M.O.M.S. idea around in my head and I even started a mental list of possible steps. The concept was gelling, taking form, but I was STILL half-joking about really DOING it.

One morning while I was cleaning the house, I received a telephone call from Emily, a close friend of mine who lived about two hours away. We had become friends through our sons all through their high school years. In the early stages, we were merely the parent whom we would call to verify that what our sons told us was, in fact, true. We appreciated each other's honesty and found that we shared common values. Lots of tough love and responsible parenting, along with an equal amount of joy and pride in our children sculpted our relationship. After the graduation ceremony, we promised each other that despite the fact that both boys were going away to different colleges, we would remain close. And we did. That promise was made nearly eight years prior to this emotional cry for help.

"Oh! My Gosh! I'm SO glad you're home! You're the only one I can call to talk to about this!" she sobbed. Literally. She was crying REAL tears! "Everyone in this area knows Jim and Kathryn and her family, so if I confide in anyone around here, they'll know all of the people involved! I think Kathryn hates me, and to be perfectly honest with you right now, I'm not HER biggest fan either -- OR her mother's!"

I listened as she related her story about Kathryn's unrealistic demand that Emily and her husband create identical environments for their new grandbaby in their home and cars -- actual duplicates of what Kathryn and Jim had in their house and cars! Expensive nursery furniture -- the crib, changing table, rocking chair, dresser, wall hangings, linens, bumper pads, and even the mobile. She even strongly suggested that Emily trade in her low-profile sedan for a new, late model SUV crossover -- just like the one she herself drove -- and have the local sheriff's office inspect the installation of a duplicate car seat! Everything down to the tiniest detail had to be an exact match! In addition, Kathryn's attitude of superiority was extremely condescending and hurtful.

"Emily," she began after authoritatively clearing her throat, ". . . I thought I already TOLD you that Jimmy and I are committed to providing continuity for our daughter! It seems as though you've disregarded our wishes! If you can't abide by our decisions, then we'll be making other arrangements for her day care!" she sneered. "As you know, MY mother has already set up HER environments and she's had NO PROBLEM supporting us and our decisions, so I really don't understand what the big deal is for you!" she snapped.

If I didn't know better, I would have thought that both of Cinderella's evil step-sisters had jumped right out of the pages of that fairy tale and smack dab into the body of Emily's daughter-in-law! I could just picture her at the other end of Emily's telephone line, dressed in designer clothes, looking down her nose at fingernails freshly manicured, hair highlighted and perfectly styled, airbrushed cosmetics perfectly applied, barking orders to her minions and cruelly admonishing them if her every whim was not anticipated and fulfilled to her complete satisfaction. Even Cruella de Ville had nothing on THIS girl!

Hearing all of this made me enormously grateful that I had NO problems compared to Emily! I allowed myself some time to digest this new information, but at the same time, I tried to diffuse some of the raw emotion gushing directly from my friend's heart. Validating her pain was important, but so was helping her feel better.

"Wow! I'm a little surprised at some of those demands," I admitted, "but . . . let's just take a big deep breath and count to ten, shall we?!"

"I could count to one thousand and I'd still be this upset!" wailed Emily. "You're lucky you don't live as close to your sons as I do to mine! THEN you'd see how it is!"

"Oh! O.K. Let's change places, why don't we? You move two hours away from your son and granddaughter and then tell me you're happy with not being able to see them as often as you'd like!" I suggested, sarcasm dripping from every word. "Perhaps Kathryn is having a bad day and is just trying to share the feeling with everyone around her! Maybe she's overwhelmed with being a new mother and is just not coping well!"

After the crying stopped and the crisis passed, I jokingly told her about my idea to start a M.O.M.S. support group. She actually begged me to send her a copy of the steps I had told her about (which had yet to be committed to paper or typed into a computer document!) After our conversation ended, I thought that perhaps I really SHOULD put my ideas into some form or other. It seemed, after all, that my concept was being well received!! VERY well received!

Since becoming seriously committed to this project, I have benefitted from Step 5 one hundred fold! I no longer succumb to the temptation to engage myself in emotionally charged exchanges with my son and/or daughter-in-law that only serve to make the situations worse! Instead, I recognize the need "for a meeting." I usually pick up the phone and dial another M.O.M.S. with whom to vent.

This most recent incident had me initiating a meeting not even twenty-four hours after it occurred. I willingly donate my time every Friday from 6:00 a.m. until anywhere between 4:30 p.m. and 5:30 p.m. to watch my grandson. The hours make for a very long day with an almost-three-year-old, but I love it, and I want to think that he does too. Both my son and daughter-in-law head to their jobs and I stay at their house with their son. I always bring a large thermos of coffee, sweetened heavily with some sort of caramel or crème brulee flavored creamer, transforming the beverage into more of a coffee-flavored milk drink. Of course Parker wanted a taste, and of course, I allowed it. Once he tasted the sweet convection, however, he begged for more. Not thinking it through or realizing that caffeine is very near the top of this generation of parents' "Do Not EVER Allow" list, I poured a small amount into a sippy cup. That way, Parker would have his own cup, I would minimize the germs to which I'd be exposed, and I would enjoy the rest of the drink without interruption. Our day together continued, playing with toys, watching the rain, reading books, hiding from "monsters," and singing songs. Parker has learned his ABCs, so naturally, one of the songs was that one! Magnetic alphabet letters spotted one side of the refrigerator in no particular order. There were multiples of each letter to facilitate spelling as the child's skill level developed. We each pulled up a chair and began arranging the letters in order, singing the song as we went along. Again, not thinking things through thoroughly, I suggested placing a second G and a second P in the order. (Parker's name for me is GiGi, and he is in the middle of being potty trained, so I thought that the song lent itself to reinforcing both my name and potty training! I also thought it was just plain, old-fashioned, silly fun!) "ABCDEF GiGi," we sang,

"HIJKLMNO PeePee (in the potty!) QRS, TUV, WXY and Z! Now I know my ABCs -- next time won't you sing with me!" He laughed. I laughed ---- until incoming text messages buzzed my phone shortly after I'd returned home that evening.

"You gave Parker COFFEE??????" it read. The bold and capital letters of "coffee" and the multiple question marks emphasized my son's disapproval.

"Just the last sips of mostly vanilla creamer," I explained, knowing I'd done something wrong.

"Ok. There was some in his sippy cup last week and I forgot to talk to you about that. No coffee for him please . . . he's wound up enough as it is. But thank you for watching him," he admonished in the next message.

"Ok. Got it. Sorry about that!!!" I texted, finishing the exchange. (I'd hoped that the multiple exclamation points would be as emphatic to my apology as his repeated question marks were to his reprimand!)

My husband passed through the family room as I busily typed into my iPhone,

"Who are you texting?" he asked.

"Tim. I'm in trouble for giving Parker coffee," I explained.

"Uh oh!" he said, "You're in the penalty box!"

I worried about my transgressions for the rest of the evening and into the next morning. Scenes of the prior day replayed in my mind! Parker had sung the modified ABC song with the double Gs and Ps for his daddy. Tim made little comment at the time, but now I felt that I should have just left well enough alone and NOT played around with the song at all. Pouring myself a second cup of coffee reminded me of yesterday's faux pas, allowing Parker to have some.

Should I text Tim and Kristen this morning, apologizing again? I wondered, *Or should I just leave things the way they are?*

Not knowing WHAT to do about that, I DID know how to take care of myself! I called a friend (also a mother of two married sons) and told her my tale of woe.

"Eleanor, I'm in the penalty box," I told her. "I gave Parker some coffee yesterday."

"Uh oh," she began, "caffeine to our kids is one of the worst things you can give their children!"

After a lengthy conversation, I asked her whether or not I should send a follow-up text apology. Together we decided that I should just move forward. I'd already apologized.

Throughout the day, I told my story to two other M.O.M.S. Both of them told me that they cherished the memories they had of drinking coffee with their grandmothers!

"I used to drink coffee with MY grandma ALL THE TIME! She used to put honey and milk in it for me! I LOVED IT!" my friend, Heidi said.

Jackie, the other confessor, remarked, "Oh my gosh! My grandmother used to sprinkle cinnamon in my coffee! I don't remember whether or not my mom disapproved or not, but I LOVED spending my time with THAT grandma!"

Leaning on my friends allowed me to own my responsibility for offering my grandson some "forbidden fruit," and it also took some of the sting away from being in the "penalty box." Step 5 is SO important!

The 12 Steps of M.O.M.S. recently became the topic of conversation at a cocktail party where a man who had single-parented two daughters asked for a copy of my steps! He shared many of the same feelings I had about being ousted from No. 1 position in my son's life as he had being ousted from No. 1 male position in his daughters' lives when they became engaged! (Perhaps there's another 12-Step Program yet to be created under the umbrella of M.O.M.S.: D.A.D.S. -- Dads and Daughters' Spouses!) WHO KNEW that an idea that began as an off-the-cuff sarcastic remark had the power to positively influence so many people?! I am extremely excited to "pay it forward" to as many of us M.O.M.S. (and D.A.D.S.) out there that I possibly can! We are all in this together!

Step 6: Forgive All Family (and Extended Family) Members Who Have Innocently and Unintentionally Stepped on Your Feelings. Do NOT harbor ill will.

"When you forgive, you love.

And when you love, God's light shines upon you"

--John Krakauer, <u>Into the Wild</u>

How fitting it is that such inspirational words spring from John Krakauer's best-selling book, "Into the Wild," for it is truly into wild, uncharted territory that M.O.M.S. wander! Christopher Columbus, Amerigo Vespucci, Ponce De Leon and Lewis & Clark are mere amateurs in comparison to mothers of married sons. All of those pioneers in exploration endured inclement weather, rugged terrain, possible malnutrition, beriberi and other health hazards that impeded their journeys. M.O.M.S. traverse across, through, over, under, around, among, behind, beneath, inside and above the dangerous, delicate Land of Emotion! They are the captains of their ships, the leaders of their expeditions, but they're out there alone without a crew! There is no REI, Dick's, army surplus store or any other sporting goods store, in any city that stocks supplies for this sort of deployment -- NONE!

M.O.M.S. are immediately and unwittingly thrust into rigorous, intensive, doctoral level curricula of psychology the minute their sons "pop the question!" There have been no textbooks, no study manuals or class notes, no professors or counselors and no study groups --- until now. But fear not! The cavalry has arrived! This 12-Step Guide for Mothers of Married Sons offers support, encouragement and methods for all sojourns into The Land of Emotion. Novice and veteran travelers alike can benefit from studying and working the Steps. More experienced travelers shepherd the neophytes, listening and encouraging. At the same time the more senior members work with the freshmen to strengthen their own commitments to the program. Collectively, the crew steers its own ship across the choppy, tumultuous seas of The Land of Emotion and avoids catastrophic dangers hidden below.

Just as Christopher Columbus encountered unforeseen incidents during his voyages, M.O.M.S. also face many complications with increasing the size of their families by just one single daughter-in-law. The simple question uttered by a son to his future wife, "Will you marry me?" ignites the launch sequence of exploding emotions -- his, hers, yours, your family's and her family's! With all of those free-flying feelings flapping through the air, it is no wonder that emotional confusion and chaos ensue. Because mothers of married sons love their sons so deeply, intensely and unconditionally, it is crucial that they embody the entire definition of that profound love which includes forgiveness.

Forgiveness is a gift that M.O.M.S. give to themselves. It is empowering; it is uplifting and it releases bitterness. Most importantly, it allows the forgiver to live a life of joy. First and foremost, every mother of a married son should bestow forgiveness upon herself. In that one act, she begins to adjust her attitude and change her outlook, ultimately laying the groundwork for a new iteration of her role as a mother -- and mother-in-law. Some may bristle at this suggestion, for traditionally, mothers of married sons have subscribed to the notion that it is they who have been wronged by others! Why would there be a need to forgive themselves first?

The following list offers possible suggestions, for starters. Mothers of married sons should forgive themselves for:

1. Resisting/refusing to acknowledge that the relationship with their sons has/will change. It is supposed to change -- it does not mean that his love for his mother has died!
2. Failing to realize that their sons are taking a wife and that wife now occupies #1 position in his life.
3. Expecting holidays and other family gatherings to continue as if there had been no addition to the family.

4. Imposing their own desires and expectations onto the new couple. Initially the danger lies with the wedding preparations. Later on it could take other forms, such as where the couple will live, how the couple will discipline, educate, raise their children, when, how often and for how long the couple and their children will visit, etc. The issues are endless.

5. Resenting their new daughter-in-law's family and their long-standing traditions and customs.

6. Feeling superior.

7. Feeling inferior.

8. Choosing to feel insecure.

9. Choosing to be petty

10. Choosing to be inflexible.

11. Choosing manipulative behavior -- either aggressively or passive-aggressively.

Let the floodgates open! Allow forgiveness to wash away all bitterness, resentment and envy and make way for a brand new, crisp, clean, happy future relationship with your son and his wife. After mothers of married sons have forgiven themselves, they can move toward forgiving other family members (and extended family members) who may have innocently (or not so innocently) committed egregious transgressions against them!

Some M.O.M.S. may benefit from the support of close friends or other mothers of married sons to facilitate the notion of forgiveness. Phone calls, emails, video calls and personal visits are always an option. Reach out! After all, this 12-Step Program for Mothers of Married Sons was conceived because of the fact that I recognized how helpful it was for me to lean on my friends.

It wasn't long after Tim and Kristen became engaged that I began my first 3-unit intensive seminar in The Psycho-Sensory Emotional Profile of Mothers of Married Sons 101(A) -- An Introductory Course. I don't remember applying for admission or registering for the class, but there I was, enrolled and accountable for the coursework! Tim had shared his plan to propose to Kristen with me. The two had entered the Las Vegas Marathon in early March 2008, but what Kristen did NOT know was that they would not be among those running. Tim reserved a table for two at a fancy restaurant where he would propose to Kristen during dinner. He made special arrangements with the manager ahead of time for sparkling champagne to toast the occasion and he told me he'd text me afterward! My phone buzzed an incoming text from Tim well before the dinner hour.

I'm SO nervous. My hands are sweaty! it read.

I watched every minute tick by on the clock, excitedly envisioning the whole scene. Finally, after an eternity of anxious minutes, I received a second text:

She said YES!!!

Another unexpected text buzzed in just a few second later. He had sent a picture that the waiter had taken of the two of them sitting close together, clearly glowing, with Kristen's engagement ring flashing brilliantly from her ring finger!

Having been included in the proposal plans and being a part of the excitement made me feel very special. I still occupied the top spot woman in my son's life -- or so I believed! (Keep in mind, however, that the question had been "popped," and so had the launch sequence of exploding emotions! I just didn't know about that part of it at the time!)

The invisible whirling vortex of emotion spun through both families like a Category 5 hurricane! I never saw it coming and I certainly didn't know what hit me! All of a sudden, within the next five days, invitations to an engagement party were designed and ordered, possible venues for both the wedding AND the reception were listed, bridal registries were created and even a TimandKristen website had been designed and posted on the Web! The site even streamed their favorite love songs while professionally shot photographs of the happy couple cascaded across the home page! A website??? REALLY???!!! Professional photos??? SERIOUSLY???!!! Plans for two wedding showers had already begun and guest lists were being finalized. I was literally dumbstruck. Speechless. Shell-shocked! And SO not in control! There had hardly been time to enjoy hearing all the details about the proposal, and now a storm of events and details pummeled me like cannon balls! The leather bound family Bible that I purchased and hand-signed and dated as a celebratory engagement gift seemed inadequate in comparison to the epic gala affairs that were quickly unfolding!

My husband and I met Tim, Kristen and Kristen's mother at Ruth's Chris for dinner on Saturday night --- one week after Tim's proposal -- to formally celebrate the betrothal. The evening was lovely. The expression on my son's face every time he looked at his bride-to-be told me that he had chosen for love. Kristen's mother was absolutely genuine and down to earth. My heart felt happy and my instincts assured me that this marriage would be a good one. Of course, the dinner conversation revolved around the impending dervish of exciting upcoming events. As I listened, my internal cash register busily rang up dollar amount after dollar amount with the total continuing to rise into the scary range -- and we hadn't even factored in the rehearsal dinner or the honeymoon yet! Suddenly, my yen for a rich, gooey dessert and a demitasse of port vanished. All I could stomach now was a tablespoon of Pepto Bismol or Mylanta! Almost apologetically, I presented my modest engagement gift Bible feeling like I should have done something more, but . . . at the time of the purchase, I thought that it WAS something big! Tim and Kristen accepted the gift graciously, remarking about how it would become a family treasure. As they flipped through the pages, they said beautiful things about the Bible and even emphasized that it was even more special since it bore my handwriting. Their gratitude and grace touched me. However, something undefined tugged from deep within me. Was it my subconscious recognition that my son had "moved on?" Was he "leaving" me? I felt suddenly alone -- like I had been swept away by a very strong riptide into this planet's sixth (and deepest) ocean: The Nuptial!

"Wow!" I cried to my husband on the drive home following dinner, "Can you beLIEVE all the hoopla that's being planned for BEFORE they even get married? I mean . . . have you ever heard of so many parties, showers, luncheons and tastings before? The engagement party they're planning sounds like it's going to be just as fancy as the wedding reception! Then there are the wedding showers!"

"Every family has different ways of celebrating!" he answered.

"But . . . gosh! Did you do any of the math? It's going to be sooooooooo expensive!" I continued.

"It'll all work out!" he said, like he ALWAYS did! It should be noted that answers such as, "It'll all work out, "It's not a big deal!" and "Life's too short!" are Michael's default responses to me each time I traverse into The Land of Emotion. They are his way of attempting to diffuse my hyper manic overreactions to things that surprise me. What he has yet to figure out is that they are as abrasive to me as the sound of fingernails from BOTH hands scratching down a chalkboard!

Days and weeks passed with party planning in full flurry and me increasingly overwhelmed by the remarkable thoroughness and attention to detail shown by Kristen and her family in preparing for . . . EVERYTHING -- and with me also feeling less and less significant! A few of my friends snickered at my lengthy descriptions of all that was forthcoming, saying, "Hey -- you're the mother of the groom. All you're supposed to do is 'shut up and wear beige!'"

What should have registered as part of my new role (but didn't) were the words "shut up and wear beige!" My first assignment at being the Mother of the Groom was to "shut up?" "Shut up" as in "be quiet," "don't say anything," which translates into "You are SOOOOOOOO not important anymore!" For the immediately preceding twenty-seven years, my voice was THE voice, the IMPORTANT, DECISION-MAKING voice, and now I was supposed to "shut up!" Who are THEY to tell me to "shut up?" Well -- "they" hadn't told me to "shut up!" "They" had actually invited me to participate in their planning. "They" had been lovely. Luckily, I was savvy enough to recognize that I had lost control of my composure. In an effort to rein myself in before I embarrassed and/or humiliated myself AND my son, I ran straight to a bookstore for a guidebook for mothers of grooms! I really didn't think any such books existed, but was delighted to find two or three on the shelf from which to choose! I bought them all!! Dog-eared and worn from constant usage, I studied these manuals almost as thoroughly as theologians study the Bible!

I have forgiven myself for reacting the way I did. I have forgiven my newly acquired in-law family for innocently stepping on my feelings. I have forgiven my husband for his customary default responses.. My ship still sails across The Nuptial and there are still dangers afloat, but my attention to the Steps and my willingness to focus on MY attitude makes my journey one of joy.

Step 7: Flatter Your Daughter-In-Law

and Genuinely MEAN IT!

"In the best, the friendliest and simplest relations flattery or praise is necessary, just as grease is necessary to keep wheels turning."

— Leo Tolstoy, <u>War and Peace</u>

As I worked through the newly-crafted 12-Steps of M.O.M.S., it was essential that I live each step, one day at a time, as prescribed by such programs. The longer I worked it, the easier it got. Vestiges of the Old Me shrank, little by little, as the Steps imbedded more firmly into my daily routine. I became less rigid in my expectations. I looked at myself with new eyes. Was the way I did things REALLY the best way? The ONLY way? Absolutely not! Would it hurt me to acknowledge that my daughters-in-law had shown me that there were several ways to the same end? Absolutely not! Would it be fun to validate -- out loud -- that they did something terrific? Absolutely!

Tim and Kristen had been searching to buy a house for an eternity. Property values in Los Angeles County are among the highest in the nation, making it extremely difficult for young people to leverage themselves into the market. Since Tim works in Santa Monica, their initial plan was to find a home within a fifteen to twenty mile radius. That range soon widened, and kept further expanding into areas farther and farther away. They began accepting the notion of longer commutes versus affordable housing, which took them miles and miles away from living near any family members. They knew they wanted to be near relatives but being near family and owning a house seemed to be an unattainable dream. At long last, however, they did find a house -- close to many members of Kristen's family, and stretched to make the purchase.

A house! THEIR house! But that house was one with a great deal of "deferred maintenance" and one that required significant updating and TLC. As I so often do, I reached back into my memory store for the time I was a young married woman with my first house and a baby. I recalled lavish plans to make my house the envy of the entire neighborhood. *Architectural Digest* would court me, asking to feature my house in its magazine. The California Landscape Contractors Association would endow me with its award for beautification. Yes -- my house would be the most beautiful one -- ever. Dreams are wonderful, indeed. Reality, however, put a few of those dreams on hold. Other priorities arose: car payments, student loan payments, pediatrician visits, and childcare and then ultimately, the financial strain of becoming a single mother. While I was very excited that Tim and Kristen had found a house (and one so close to family support) I questioned how long it would take for them to give it the homey feeling they talked about.

Each time I visited, I noticed several home improvement projects in various stages of completion. Splotches of different colored paint samples competed for attention, each one vying to become the favorite in Kristen's eyes. The decision finally made, one wall covered in either a bold teal or turquoise reigned supreme over the warmth of the other three walls' various shades of taupes and greys. Crisp, white, glossy crown molding crept further and further around each corner of the ceilings, creating a definite regal feeling. Light fixtures -- a contemporary chandelier and sconces -- defined Kristen's decorating style as an eclectic balance of blending the staid traditional with the simple, functional modern motifs. Special attention to smaller details also changed this house into a home. Plain, ordinary doorknobs were replaced with equally functional ones but they had real style. Drab, chipped, outdated tile in the faux fireplace was torn out in favor of an original inlaid and intricate mosaic designed especially for that living room by Kristen herself! Week after week I sat in that room finding myself both charmed by the welcoming feeling of the home and intrigued by the choice of color and how well they collaborated. In fact, as I enjoyed the view from the sofa, I mentally repainted the rooms in my own house, choosing a bright, bold color to "pop" my rooms too! If emulation is the ultimate form of flattery, then my thoughts demonstrated it to the "nth" degree! I could not confine my admiration for the wondrous transformation I had witnessed in that "fixer upper!"

"Kristen -- I am SO impressed with how fantastic this house looks! I honestly would have NEVER thought to pair some of these colors that you have chosen, but I've got to tell you . . . it looks fabulous!" I gushed.

"Thanks!" Kristen replied, "I've been looking through magazines and talking to an interior designer. That's how I got some of these ideas!"

"Well, even so . . . an idea is an idea, but you brought it to life!" I continued.

I am still always eager to go to their house, not only because I love them and want to see them, but also because I honestly can't wait to see what they've recently done to the house and yard (and to secretly see how I can adapt it to MY house and yard!)

My other daughter-in-law, Lacey, is also a gem. Old Me shrinks and shrivels -- as well she should -- when her rigid expectations and judgments are squelched by Lacey's genuine charm. Old Me is now nothing but a thing of the past.

It was during our Christmas trip to Hawaii to visit Drew and Lacey that Old Me was dealt her fatal blow! I don't really know WHAT I expected simply because being entertained by my adult married children was so new at the time. What I DID know was that, in MY experience, Christmas Dinner was a full-blown formal event. The best linens draped over the dining room table. Specially folded embroidered napkins perched on the table, guarding each place setting as stiff and straight as military sentries. Bone china plates, coffee cups and saucers, intricately etched crystal goblets, sterling silver flatware and specially-ordered centerpieces from the florist were the standard for this once-a-year special evening meal. Old Me also knew that Drew and Lacey never registered for any of this finery at the time of their wedding, so I knew they had none. I am ashamed to admit this, but I'm pretty sure that Old Me was just waiting to see what kind of Christmas dinner presentation lay ahead. Segments of Chevy Chase's 1989 spoof film, "Christmas Vacation," replayed in my mind over and over and over. I couldn't decide whether I wanted to be Beverly D'Angelo's character, Ellen Griswold, or if I should just remain a non-participatory observer! Lucky for me, I drew upon my newly crafted 12-Step Guide for M.O.M.S. and invoked Step 7: Flatter Your Daughter-in-Law and Genuinely MEAN It! I consciously banished Old Me's judgmental tendencies in favor of the slogan, "Live and Let Live," and am I ever glad I did! Locking Old Me in a box and throwing away the key is the best gift I have ever given - both to my sons AND to myself!

Christmas 2012 can officially be entered in my biography as The Best Christmas of My Life. With Old Me gone and out of the way, I felt a tremendous burden lifted. The sky was bluer, the birds chirped louder, the ocean was clearer and even the air was warmer. I became lighter, physically and spiritually, and happiness dominated the entire island of Oahu (or at least our little piece of it!) We planned activities to do as a family; my husband and I babysat my grandson while my sons and their wives did things on their own; I listened as my two daughters-in-law chatted about hair and fashion, chiming in myself every now and then.

Drew and Lacey had prepared well for our visit. There was nothing that had been overlooked. A Christmas tree stood next to a window, decorated with unbreakable ornaments on the bottom few branches. Lacey anticipated that 18-month-old Parker wouldn't be able to resist playing with the tree. She was also armed with a cache of small wrapped gifts, delighting Parker with one each day. A never-ending buffet of baked goodies, chips and dips, mixed nuts, deli trays, snacks and beverages beckoned from the kitchen. Board games, playing cards, an X-Box and classic Christmas movie videos provided hours and hours of indoor evening entertainment. Everything was perfect.

On Christmas morning, after eating a hearty breakfast, we all exchanged gifts, took pictures, then retired to the family room for a day of TV football and Bing Crosby feel-good flicks. Drew and Lacey banished the rest of us from the kitchen for the rest of the day. They excused themselves and told us that they were beginning the preparations for the evening's Christmas Dinner and that there would be no interruptions allowed. From time to time, I attempted to pitch in and help but was always rebuked.

"No, Peggy!" came Lacey's gentle refusal, "Drew and I have this totally under control. You just go back into the family room and relax!"

The feeling of not helping to orchestrate a holiday meal was so foreign to me! I didn't know how to react or what kinds of emotions to allow! Was I not needed? Wanted? Useful? Those questions intensified in my head, especially when Kristen's service was requested!

"Kristen . . . could you come in here for a second, please?" I heard Lacey's voice coming from the kitchen.

Trying to remain calm, I glanced nonchalantly toward the partially closed kitchen door. Kristen emerged, carrying a loaded tray containing dinnerware, stemware, placemats and napkins. Next came Lacey. The two girls set the table together, discussing seat assignments and making decisions on which centerpiece was more suitable. At that point, I wished my ears were as big as Dumbo the Elephant's and as sharp as a jackrabbit's. I strained to hear the girls' whispered conversation, but try as I may, Bing Crosby's crooning "White Christmas" on television prevented all stealth eavesdropping! I subtly lowered the volume on the remote control just in time to hear Lacey say, "I just want everything to be SO perfect!"

And it was. I stifled the tears that were welling up in my eyes as I realized the monumental effort Lacey had made to make this a wonderful Christmas. My sweet daughter-in-law had bent over backwards, jumped through hoops and pulled out all the stops for . . . us.

And, for the record, . . . at no point was there any void because of the absence of bone china, sterling silver, fine linens or crystal goblets. They weren't missed at all!

I do remember complimenting Lacey on having gone overboard and for being a superb hostess in one of the Christmas toasts. I also penned a thank you note (written on one of my personalized Crane card stock notecards, of course!) upon my return back to the mainland, but I still didn't think I conveyed how deeply I was touched or how much I appreciated her. A few months later, on

Lacey's birthday, I sent her a text message wishing her a happy day, but also thanking her for being such a perfect wife for Drew and a very loved gift to our family.

Flattery, according to the wisdom of Leo Tolstoy, is just as necessary an ingredient in relationships as grease is to a machine. What his wisdom lacks, however, is that genuine, authentic flattery greases not only the machine, but the grease can as well!

Step 8: Do Not Complain

"You can complain because roses have thorns, or you can
rejoice because thorns have roses."

--Ziggy

The Land of M.O.M.S. is dotted with landmines. Perhaps one
of the reasons young married women cringe at the mention of the
word "mother-in-law" is because so many mothers of married sons
have been navigating through this uncharted territory for eons
without a compass, a map, a 12-step guide designed especially for
them. Mothers of married sons have fought for their sons'
expressions of love, attention, value and consideration in all the
wrong ways. Their game strategies are deeply flawed! They needle
and nag, pry and pester, whine and whimper in their desperate
attempts to hang on to their sons. What is overlooked is the fact that
they do not need to "hang on" -- they already have their sons'
love! Think of all those televised championship college football
games -- New Year's Day Rose Bowl games immediately come to my
mind. A huge beast of a lineman -- measuring well over six feet tall
and close to 300 pounds -- just sacks the quarterback, making THE
play of the game. Cameras hone in on him, reporters swarm around

and what does he do? He beams from ear to ear and yells, "Hi, Mom!"

"It would be nice to hear from you once in awhile!" or "My tuna noodle casserole was ALWAYS your favorite! When did THAT change?" or in mid-March (or even earlier) there's the common "I'm hosting Thanksgiving this year -- I'm asking early so I'm sure you'll be at our table!" And let's NOT forget the "Oh! I made these -- your favorite -- cookies for you, thinking that you'd stop by, but it's been so long now, they've gone stale!" These are admittedly annoying and we know it. Passive-aggressive manipulation has been the default strategy for centuries -- with not much success.

Step 8: Do Not Complain, introduces a new methodology, but it requires great focus and attention. Slogans from other 12-step programs, such as "It works if you work it," "One Day at a Time," "Live and Let Live" and "Expect Miracles" should become daily mantras. Support from other M.O.M.S., either on the phone, through e-mails, coffee dates or at larger group meetings serves to strengthen not only the individual, but each member of the larger group as well. M.O.M.S. can commiserate among themselves, each venting their own brand of personal pain and woe. It is their common bond. Together, M.O.M.S. can transform themselves from bitter and resentful hags into content and happy women with adult married sons. Just remember: practice makes perfect! And IT WORKS, IF YOU WORK IT!

I actively and consciously remodeled my complaining behavior through vigorous attention to the 12-step slogans and through the support of a few close friends with whom I shared my woes. Several holidays passed without one false step onto a hidden landmine. Truthfully, though, I repeatedly uttered those slogans and unloaded my angst onto my close friends non-stop for quite awhile. Eventually, however, I noticed a change in myself! I no longer had knee-jerk emotional reactions that ordinarily plummeted me into a whirling downward tailspin. If and when I made my sons' "favorite cookies," I no longer kept them at my house as bait, hoping to lure them home for a visit. I cut the recipe in half, baked the cookies, then enjoyed them with a steaming cup of hot coffee while I reminisced about fond memories of their childhoods. I did not set myself up for disappointment nor did I lay traps for my sons to visit, knowing that they wouldn't. Constant pressure from the media airing such warm holiday classics as "It's a Wonderful Life," and "The Walton Family Christmas," depicting large, loving family gatherings, peace and joy faded into more realistic approaches to my family's dynamic. Think about it: There's no way that John-Boy Walton's parents would EVER get divorced like I did! Why did I try to superimpose that ideal onto my situation? When I tossed all that aside, my life became much less complicated, and MUCH happier!

Informal meetings of M.O.M.S. rejuvenated my spirit. Of course I still fought against complaining! After all, a battleship's course cannot be redirected THAT quickly! Petty complaints fell from my lips to my friend Gayle's ears. In turn, her complaints fell to my ears. The same held true with my friend, Renee. Just the act of listening to each other helped to diffuse our urges to complain to our sons. Instead, we offered each other alternate reactions or even no reaction.

One of my greatest rewards for working the steps and not complaining came in the form of a house key! A simple house key. Tim and Kristen purchased a house within less than five miles' distance to Kristen's mother's house. Kristen's grandparents lived less than two miles away and Kristen's aunt lived approximately the same distance away in the opposite direction. I was very happy that they would have so much family close by, especially after Parker was born. New mothers always need help, and with them being so close to Kristen's mother, grandmother and aunt, she would lack for nothing! The "infantry" was strategically placed! Events in my life evolved which allowed me the opportunity to babysit one day a week. I arrived at Tim and Kristen's house very early in the morning before Kristen left for work, and I stayed late into the early evening until either Tim or Kristen arrived home. The routine worked! As Parker grew older, however, I thought it would be fun to start taking him on outings during the day. At first, I pushed him in his stroller down to a nearby park, only two blocks from the house, leaving the back door unlocked because I had no key. We scattered breadcrumbs on the grass for the ducks, geese and squirrels then watched the turtles jump from steep rocks into the pond. Knowing that I'd left the house open always nagged at me, so I kept the visits to the park short -- about thirty minutes. Subsequent adventures took us further away from home -- up to a public park with swings and playground equipment -- with the back door left unlocked for our re-entry. I mentioned how uncomfortable I felt about leaving the house vulnerable to a break-in, and Kristen understood. Subsequently, she always left her house key with me, mentioning that she should have one made for me just as she had already done for her mother. Kristen's mother having a key to their house made all sorts of sense! ME having a key to their house meant more than just having a key to their house! It meant TRUST. But months passed with no key!

"Gayle --- Kristen's mother -- has had a key to the kids' house for I don't know HOW long!" I whined during one of our informal meetings of M.O.M.S.

"So?" replied Gayle, "So what? Doesn't she live like five seconds from them? Doesn't she let the painters in and the exterminator and other workers too?"

Her logic was infuriating!

"Yes, she lives five seconds away and yes, she does all that, but SHE HAS A KEY and I DON'T!" I wailed.

"Oh! C'mon!" said Gayle, "you don't really need a key! You're just upset because Kristen's mom has something allowing her more access to Tim and Kristen and you don't!"

"You're right! She has their trust and I don't!" I moaned, knowing that I was sounding ridiculous.

"Ugh!! Just listen to yourself! You're complaining about . . . nothing! They already TRUST you! They leave a key with you when you're there and when you need it, don't they? Good grief! They leave their SON with you!" she said. "If they didn't TRUST you, you wouldn't even be babysitting!"

"I know. But . . . I think I'd just feel more . . . I don't know . . . more . . . a part of them if I had a key!" I answered.

A few more months passed with Kristen leaving her house key for me while she went to work. I said nothing about the key; I just continued to leave her key on the kitchen counter before I left to go home. Truthfully, there was nothing wrong with that arrangement! I'd vented, I practiced not complaining and I lived "one day at a time." I'd even forgotten about the key issue altogether! Life was good.

Life was good indeed, but it was on the verge of becoming GREAT! The summer months passed with the routine continuing to work. Kristen left her house key with me in the morning and I placed it on the kitchen counter on top of the day's mail in the afternoon. One particularly bright November morning, however, I met my wonderful and totally unexpected surprise! Just before Kristen left for work, she handed me a small brown bag saying,

"Oh! I almost forgot! We had this made for you and Parker picked it out!"

I turned the bag upside down. What fell into my hand was a bright Kelly green Schlage house key with red ladybugs all over it!! Fireworks and balloons lit up my sky while my heart soared in celebratory elation! I didn't have just an ordinary house key -- I have the key to happiness!

Lesson learned? Step 8: Do Not Complain challenged me to "live and let live." I came to understand that grumbling and nitpicking locks doors while acting with joy opens them. After all, I have the bright green key with ladybugs on it as proof!

Step 9: Never Put Your Son in the Middle

"A psychologist once told me that for a boy being in the middle of a conflict between two women is the worst possible situation. There's always a desire to please each one."

--Hillary Clinton

Anyone who has ever travelled for any distance occupying the middle position of the back seat of a car knows how miserably uncomfortable it is. The preformed seats, designed for the two outermost passengers, offer nothing to support the middle traveler. There are no arm rests, no bolstered lumbar supports, no soft cushions on which to sit and no leg room per se; the middle person straddles the bump that runs down the center of the vehicle -- one foot on either side of it on the floor while constantly balancing to keep the body mounted on the hard hump just beneath the upholstery. Leaning to either side yields no relief. It only creates more problems for everyone on the seat. The shoulder strap and lap belt constrict against movement too far in any sideways direction. In addition, since there is no window for the person in the center, he stares straight ahead, using the front windshield as a portal to the outside world. The middle person is a prisoner, tethered and cramped between two well-rested, relaxed companions enjoying the

100

scenes from their own private windows. No one really willingly volunteers for the middle.

Unless M.O.M.S. are vigilant in their attention to Step 9, that's exactly where their sons find themselves -- sandwiched between their wives and their mothers -- squeezed into the "mother" of no-win situations! Roads become extremely dangerous for those vehicles. Despite the numerous traffic signs warning of danger, hazardous conditions, windy roads, sharp S-curves, dead ends and slippery slopes, those cars are careening out of control toward certain doom. M.O.M.S. must stay out of the back seats of those cars; in fact, they must stay out of those cars altogether!

It is not unusual in these modern times for both members of a couple to be career-oriented. During the early years of a marriage the couple adjusts to each other's schedules, night classes, business trips and overtime hours, feeding that ambition. M.O.M.S. flutter along the periphery, enjoying their sons' success and professional advancements. They are also very proud of their daughters-in-law, bragging about them whenever they get the chance.

"My son, Brian, just made junior partner at his law firm after only two years!" and "Denise, my daughter-in-law, is a fashion stylist to the Hollywood stars! She'll be dressing Julia Roberts for this year's Oscars! Isn't that fabulous?" gushed from my friend's lips. My friend Taylor couldn't have been more pleased. I listened as she poured out an elaborate description of Denise's glamorous life. Trips to New York City "to see and be seen" was part of her daughter-in-law's job. The more exposure she had to the celebrities, the more likely she was to be hired by them as their sole personal stylist. She shopped on 5th Avenue, attended the fashion shows of all the top designers and hobnobbed with "the beautiful people." Taylor's daughter-in-law certainly had it going in a big way, that's for sure. What a dream job!

Time passed, careers expanded, and twin children were born -- Taylor's grandchildren. At this point in time Brian had become a full partner in his law firm and Denise was one of the most sought-after stylists among Hollywood's royalty! While Denise was still on maternity leave, Taylor gingerly asked her son about childcare, desperately hoping against hope that she'd get the answer she knew she would never hear:

"Childcare? What do you mean, childcare? Denise is going to stay home with the kids!"

If Taylor could have been blessed with immediate deafness, she would have never had suffered the blistering pain of hearing the plans for her grandchildren's care.

"Denise has already been interviewing nannies because she's contracted with Jennifer Aniston for the Golden Globes," explained Brian. "I, personally, would prefer it if she went on a sabbatical until the kids are school aged, but . . . she's worked so hard to get to this level and now the big actresses are seeking her out, so . . ." he continued.

"WHAT!?" Taylor shrieked, accidentally betraying her disapproval. "Hollywood starlets and FASHION take precedence over Marcus and Angela?"

"Yes, well . . . when you put it that way, it sounds worse than it is!" Brian answered. "A big part of me agrees with you. I would truly love it if Denise stayed home and did the full-time mother thing, I really would. But you know, she and I have BOTH worked really hard to build our careers, and she'll be making really good money. Paying for full time nannies won't be a burden."

"But if you really want her to take some time off, you should speak up and be a little more assertive! These are your children we're talking about here -- not last year's fashion trend! Children need their mothers!" Taylor insisted.

Over a cup of coffee at the kitchen table, mother and son tugged back-and-forth for quite some time weighing the two opposing attitudes regarding career pursuits and parenting responsibilities. Up until the thump of a large handbag on the kitchen floor announced her return, neither Taylor nor Brian realized that Denise had overheard their entire exchange. Heads turned, jaws dropped and Brian looked as guilty as if he'd been caught having an affair with one of Denise's Hollywood clients! He immediately stammered a pathetic explanation.

"Hi, Honey! Uh . . . I didn't know you were home! Uh . . . my mom and I were just discussing your upcoming return to work and nannies and . . ."

"STOP!" Denise hissed through tightly clenched teeth, so low she was hardly audible. "This conversation between the two of us is SO not over!"

The angry glare from her eyes burned through mother and son as she pivoted and turned down the hallway. The air in the room instantly plummeted to sub-arctic temperatures. The sky darkened and deafening silence roared throughout the house. Not even a minute later a slam from the master bedroom door crashed through the house, intensifying the tension.

"O.K.," whispered Taylor, "I'm going to go now, but remember what I said! You can NEVER get back time NOT spent with your children. You even told me it's what YOU wanted!" And with that, another door slammed, leaving Brian stunned and staring straight ahead from the tightly constrictive middle seat!

Road signs, barricades and flashing warning lights couldn't keep that car from freefalling over a cliff that day. Taylor's righteousness and unabashed disdain over her son and daughter-in-law's plans propelled her future relationship with her daughter-in-law past any body shop straight into the salvage yard.

Whoever said "time heals all wounds" was way off the mark! Eight years have passed since Taylor's grandchildren were born and no more than eight words have been exchanged between Taylor and her daughter-in-law in that same amount of time. Brian and the twins visit Taylor from time to time and there are phone calls and video chats among the three of them, but disharmony prevails between Denise and her husband's mother. Taylor has extended several olive branches -- enough to plant an entire forest, in fact, -- but Denise remains icy and detached.

"I have nothing against women pursuing careers," Taylor explained in one of her apologies. "I KNOW that times have changed and that many young mothers pursue their careers. I am so sorry that I imposed my philosophy onto you and Brian! I was wrong! Won't you please forgive me?"

Taylor and Denise had never been comfortable with each other prior to this cataclysmic collapse of their relationship. It was polite and civil, but personality differences, attitudes and geographical distance presented obstacles over which neither one could hurdle. This one unfortunate lapse in Taylor's judgment -- putting her son in the middle between his wife and his mother -- cost her dearly. Even though a truce has been declared, the relationship between the two of them remains badly scarred. On a few occasions, Denise has accompanied her family on their visits to Taylor's house, but she does not engage in conversation or participate in any of the family activities. Instead, she pores through fashion magazines, searches the internet on her laptop computer and concentrates on finding the perfect styles for her famous clients. Mother and daughter-in-law share only one thing: their love for Brian, Marcus and Angela.

Travelling at high speeds with a backseat full of explosives can only lead to a catastrophic collision. Taylor, of course, regrets having pushed her son into the middle seat and wishes she had never belted in at all. When the hairpin turns along the way forced him off balance, he leaned in his wife's direction (as he should) -- and when that car ultimately crashed, Taylor found herself dazed at impact and thrown from the vehicle.

I am grateful to Taylor for leaning on me during this event in her life. This is exactly what the M.O.M.S. program is designed for: to support and guide each other through certain behaviors that will lead to happiness and well-being. Taylor's struggle has saved me from treading on similar dangerous ground myself! Her tragic tale helped me focus on myself and my own attitudes, expectations and opinions and encouraged me to remove all of that codependent baggage from my budding new role as a Mother of a Married Son. I believe that had I not committed to creating this 12-Step Program for Mothers of Married Sons, this story would have remained locked in Taylor's hidden box of regrets. Other M.O.M.S., too, may have fallen victim to a similar nuclear meltdown by putting their sons in the middle seat.

Whether or not a young mother should return to work after having children is really not the issue. After all, hundreds of thousands of mothers hold jobs and parent their children quite effectively and efficiently. If in doubt, look to the growing number of working single mothers. M.O.M.S. must respect the decisions that their sons and daughters-in-law make that are theirs -- and theirs alone -- to make. Reliance on the Steps, the Serenity Prayer, the slogans and meetings are here to help. And . . . don't forget: put a close M.O.M.S. friend on your phone's speed dial and call 1-800-S-P-O-N-S-O-R!

Step 10: Do Not Be A Doormat

"I've learned that you shouldn't go through life with a catcher's mitt
on both hands; you need to be able to throw something back."

- Maya Angelou

Sports jargon makes perfect metaphors for some of Life's
challenges. Maya Angelou uses catcher's mitts and baseballs to
encourage people to defend themselves against being
victimized. How often have you been told to "drop back ten yards
and punt" or "just put it through the uprights?" Have you ever been
thrown a "curveball?" Words of encouragement and perseverance
are often paralleled to the bottom half of the ninth inning with two
outs and bases loaded. We hear sports phrases used all the
time: "Don't stop now! There are still seconds on the clock!" or
"Play like you're already ahead!" and "It's not over 'til it's
over!" But, so many of us M.O.M.S. don't want to rock the boat in
our relationships with our sons and daughters-in-law. We unwittingly
find ourselves placed on the B Team. Our team spirit remains
strong, but our time on the field is minimal, at best. We neglect our
value in deference to "family harmony." THAT NEEDS TO
CHANGE. We should not be complacent to sit on the bench, never
to be put into the game. We, too, are integral players. We may no

longer own the team, and in fact, we most certainly don't even manage it anymore, but we still fit into the uniform and we still show up ready to play on game day! We must never forget that!

While M.O.M.S. grew and developed through its gestation period, Life continued. Both of my sons married, bought houses, grew into their careers and planned families of their own. I drifted with the tides in my new role as a M.O.M.S., never certain about how to express MY desires, hopes or feelings in blending families together. Life happened *to* me. Decisions were made, plans were carried out and, because I hesitated to contribute my voice, I became an unwilling doormat. I convinced myself that some things were "no big deal," and not worth creating conflict over. But finally there was that proverbial straw that broke the camel's back.

I had successfully navigated my way through my sons' dating, engagements and both weddings with admirable aplomb, if I do say so myself. With my budding 12-Steps constantly on my mind, I practiced Step 3: Keep Your Mouth Shut with regularity. Most of the time it paid off. But then again, most of the time the issues were small and insignificant. THEN . . . Kristen got pregnant.

I had not yet assimilated to my demotion in rank to "mother-in-law," and I was suddenly facing having to define myself again as a grandmother!! Of course I was beyond over-the-moon with excitement, who wouldn't be?! Being a grandmother would most assuredly be a breeze! Not at ALL like becoming a mother-in-law! I anticipated all the precious moments I'd spend watching my grandchild grow; I envisioned myself reading books to him or her, trips to the zoo and many many many other happy things. It's normal. Also in line with normal reactions upon being told that your son is to become a father, I drove straight to a knit shop to purchase baby yarn with which to knit a baby blanket. It didn't bother me in the least that no one knew the sex of the baby; I chose a skein of variegated yarn containing a mixture of ALL the pastel baby colors. It's a wonder that I escaped being pulled over for speeding! I couldn't get home fast enough to begin my first project as a grandmother! Cast on 60 stitches; knit 2, slip 1, knit 1, slip 1, Turn and repeat to desired length!

The problem with being a first time grandmother (on the paternal side as we M.O.M.S. find ourselves) is that our rank as "mother-in-law" is above that of grandma. We are not privy to any of the exciting details concerning the pregnancy. We only know what trickles down to us through our sons -- which isn't much! All of the talking heads on the evening News programs talk about the severe drought that California faces due to a lack of rain. Let me tell you -- California's scant rainfall is a virtual monsoon compared to the amount of information a M.O.M.S. receives about her daughter-in-law's prenatal activity! Unlike clouds that are seeded by machines to induce rainfall, a M.O.M.S. subtle questioning of her son can't even prime the pump and begin the flow of even the tiniest of details!

"How's Kristen feeling?" I asked.

"Fine," came the reply I was afraid I'd get.

<*Ugh!*> "Is she having morning sickness?" came another attempt.

"A little," said Tim.

"Has she felt the baby move yet?" I tried one more time.

"Don't know," he replied.

Now . . . I KNOW my son is well-educated! I paid tuition for twelve years of private school education for him, he graduated from a very prestigious four-year university, then attended the London School of Economics, so I am positive that he can communicate in sentences longer than one and two syllables! I was also one-hundred percent sure that my Co-Mother-in-Law (Kristen's mom) was getting a full-length, minute-by-minute description of every twinge, pain, flutter and gas bubble on a daily basis. I summoned all of my internal strength to suppress the green-eyed monster and behave with dignity -- like a M.O.M.S. should. What I DID learn, however, was that

Kristen's family practices a plethora of traditions . . . that canNOT
be broken short of a papal dispensation. I learned about holiday
commitments early on: Christmas Eve MUST be spent at Kristen's
mother's house. Same for Easter Sunday. Thanksgiving is spent at
Kristen's aunt's house, always. I'm sure there is protocol for
Valentine's Day, Martin Luther King Day, President's Day,
Columbus Day, Halloween and all the others. None of that bothered
me . . . much. M.O.M.S. come in a little further down on the food
chain and on the list of places to be on holidays. I got that, loud and
clear.

BUT . . . Kristen's family also has a hard and fast tradition for
naming new members of the family. If the baby is a girl, the parents
choose the first name and the middle name is that of the maternal
grandmother. If the baby is a boy, again, the parents get to choose
the first name, but the middle name is that of the paternal
grandfather. All of that sounds lovely and beautiful. Usually.
However, when the paternal grandfather is a person who actually
brought a legal civil action at the time of his divorce from his sons'
mother for the wrongful lives of his children in what can only be
assumed to have been a convoluted attempt to avoid having to pay
child support; when the paternal grandfather is physically and
emotionally abusive, it is time to break with "tradition" and select a
name for that baby boy that is chosen for someone who is honorable,

112

moral, ethical and decent. Not to mention that a little consideration for MY feelings would have been . . . should have been heeded.

One beautiful, warm, sunny spring day, I was enjoying a very good round of golf -- better than I had played in a long, long time. After the first nine holes, I often check my cell phone for emails and/or text messages. It is really a very bad habit because there is never anything of urgency in my inbox that can't wait another two hours for attention. And so it was on this particular beautiful, warm, sunny Spring day. I checked my e-mails and opened one from my son, the baby's father.

"Dear Mom," it began, "you have always been a constant in my life and I deeply admire and respect you for that."

Hmmmmm . . . . this is weird! I thought.

I kept reading the note only to learn that because of the strong family tradition of naming babies, that my grandson . . . MY grandson (in the event the baby were a boy, that is) would carry the name of my sociopathic, abusive ex-husband . . . because "it's a strong tradition in Kristen's family!"

My mind exploded! My heart instantly plummeted like a giant anchor straight through the bottoms of my cleats. Tears streamed down my cheeks like raging rivers. I simply could NOT believe that a beautiful, innocent NEW life would bear the stain of a morally corrupt man's name!

How COULD he???!!!!! How COULD Tim allow such a travesty?! He KNOWS what kind of person his father is and he is going to allow "tradition" to dictate?! And while I'm at it . . . WHAT ABOUT MY FEELINGS?!!!!!! What makes Kristen's family with all of its traditions better than MY feelings?!!!

Needless to say, I did not continue on to play the back nine holes. Golf was over for the day. I could not have been more hurt had I been hung upside down, tarred, feathered and beaten with flaming hot ropes. I cried until there was nothing left. Still . . . because I understood that being a M.O.M.S. involved "keeping your mouth shut" and "not complaining," I somehow managed to type a response to Tim:

"The naming of children is 100% the parents' prerogative. They are your children. Anyone else's input is irrelevant."

. . .and I clicked the SEND button. No "Love, Mom." No "Talk to you soon!" No "xxx/ooo." Nothing. It took more strength than I had just to type out that response! I spent the remainder of the day sobbing underneath a blanket, curled in a fetal position. Internal arguments ensued between my "keep your mouth shut" self and my "don't be a doormat" self:

It's just a 5-letter name -- and it's the middle name. Who uses the middle name?

You're right! It IS a 5-letter name! Names STAND for something! Those 5 letters stand for something that is just unacceptable, that's what!! For cryin' out loud -- YOU use YOUR middle name! You can't just dust this one away! This IS important!! SAY SOMETHING!!

And so it went . . . all night long. The following morning, after an entirely sleepless night, I crawled to the computer with a fresh box of Kleenex and created a new email document to my son:

"Dear Tim: I have been up, wide awake all night, distressed about your plans to bestow the baby with your father's name should it be a boy. I truly hope it's a girl! I know that my initial response to you gave my tacit approval, but that was a lie. I abHOR the idea. It is wrong and it is beyond hurtful. I canNOT believe that you would allow such a thing. Of ALL the male names in the world . . . no!..in the UNIVERSE . . . you couldn't choose one with more honor associated with it? I am shattered to know that Kristen's family's traditions trump my feelings . . . and what's right. I know you're going to do what you're going to do, but I will NOT allow this one to go by without my input.

Mom"

I received no response for several days. Finally the other shoe dropped. My cell phone buzzed an incoming call from Tim. Neither one of us was friendly. He directed his anger at my having lied to him with my initial response. He said that he KNEW I wasn't telling the truth and that was upsetting to him.

Really!? YOU'RE upset?!! Good Grief!!!

I told him that, because of the nature of his overly-sweet email to me, explaining Kristen's strong family traditions all the while weaving in his love, admiration, appreciation and respect for me, I KNEW he was trying to sugar-coat some sort of bullet that lay beneath the loving words. There was no way around the fact that what he was prepared to allow (should the baby be a boy) was just wrong -- plain and simple. I told him that I had been trying to be an exemplary mother-in-law and stay out of their lives. THAT was the reason for my initial response. More words were exchanged, but the phone call ended with no resolution of the problem. It was a very cold, dark and sad time for us both.

One of the other Steps, Step 9: Never Put Your Son in the Middle, had just reared its head. Was I guilty of doing just that? Was I really asking my son to make a decision based on a conflict of

116

opinions between his mother and his wife? Some may argue yes. I beg to differ. At no time did I make a demand. At no time did I vilify my daughter-in-law. My son KNEW that the baby-naming tradition would become an issue for me in the event his child was born a male. He also understood that HE had to make a difficult decision. I believe that he'd expected me to be upfront and truthful with him in my initial response. He EXPECTED that from me.

My issue was multi-faceted. I KNOW that my son loves me deeply. I KNOW that he tries to do the right thing. He married into a very strong family. He was conflicted, not because of anything I had done, but because of his newly-acquired family traditions. He was a victim of circumstance.

Time passed with no further mention of the baby's middle name. In fact, communication between us was thin, anorexic even -- until Kristen went into labor!

"Kristen's in labor. We're heading to the hospital! See you there!" announced the incoming text.

Several hours later, with all the key players present in the hospital waiting room, my thoughts haunted me. The issue of the baby's middle name screamed inside my head as I tried to engage in pleasant conversation. Minutes passed like hours and hours passed like years! Finally, after an eternity of nervous but excited anticipation, all of our cell phones buzzed simultaneously:

"We'd like to announce the birth of our son, Parker ANDREW!"

They had chosen the PERFECT middle name for their son! They named him for Tim's brother!

Everyone relaxed into blissful celebration and enormous relief that there had been no complications with the birth. I literally melted into my seat. Oh, I cried tears of blissful celebration, all right, but they were MUCH more than that. My tears were definitely those of joy for the new healthy life that blessed my family. Moreover, they were also heartfelt tears for the name that this little boy had been given. It is a name of great dignity and honor -- definitely something that he can be proud of!

Had I NOT spoken up about my strong opposition to the tradition of naming babies, Tim and I both would have regretted it. Ultimately we each did the right thing: I was not a doormat and my son bent family tradition, choosing the middle name of that of his own beloved brother! Thank Goodness I listened to Maya Angelou's wisdom and took the catcher's mitt off of one of my hands! In the ninth inning of THIS game, I caught the line drive with bases loaded and hurled that ball back to home plate for a triple play!

Step 11: Be the Change You Want to See in the World (of Mothers-in-Law)

"If you don't like something, change it. If you can't change it, change your attitude."

--Maya Angelou

The Old Me ordered the world in the ways I thought it should be ordered. The Old Me structured everything according to very rigid and unbending guidelines -- mine. The way I had done things in the past was the way things should continue to be done in the future. That's just the way it was. After all, my way had worked for me, so it must be right! If I wrote thank-you notes no later than one day after receiving a gift, I expected the same from my boys. If I rinsed dishes (more like WASHED dishes) before putting them in the dishwasher, then I thought EVERYONE should do it that way too! If I used fine china for holiday dinners, I assumed, again, that EVERYONE else did too! That's just what people did! The New Me, however, has learned an invaluable lesson! The New Me has taken Maya Angelou's words to heart. The New Me has changed my attitude! It is without a doubt the most productive thing to do to enhance the new role as a M.O.M.S. Sometimes it becomes necessary to enact change in yourself, and that's when Step 11: Be the Change You Want to See in the World (of Mothers-in-Law!) should be applied. Be flexible and open-minded!

One can never anticipate what dark clouds of unexpected change loom ahead before a son becomes engaged and wedding preparations begin. We M.O.M.S. unconsciously assume that the young bride-to-be will follow the same customary traditions and practices as we did when we got married. She'll choose china, crystal, silver and linens and register her choices at two or three of the better stores; of course, the invitations will be engraved on the finest grade of stationary, and naturally, Emily Post will beam her approval at the level of formality involved from the wedding announcements through the ceremony then all the way through to the thank you notes. If the wedding is to take place before noon, the groomsmen will be in morning coats; an afternoon or evening wedding will require black tuxedos complete with bow ties and cummerbunds. Naturally. That's just how it is. Until it isn't!

Drew FINALLY decided to propose to Lacey. He asked me to accompany him to the jewelry store to help him select the perfect ring! During that time, Drew, a USMC officer, shared his 3-step plan:

1)   He'd ask Lacey to marry him;

2)   He'd serve his nine-month term in Afghanistan scheduled for the upcoming October;

3)   While he was gone, Lacey would plan the wedding and they'd marry shortly following his return.

Sounded good! Engaged for a year, then get married. But what's that saying about "the best laid plans of mice and men?"

Drew popped the question during an afternoon hike along the cliffs of Torrey Pines State Park sometime in March. Before anyone in the family could even turn around once, Lacey had confirmed a wedding date at the Admiral Kidd Club in San Diego with a non-refundable deposit for September 18 -- just weeks before Drew's deployment! There was no way Lacey was going to wait a year to become "Mrs. Drew!" How could a formal wedding be properly planned in less than six months? While I frantically poured through my previously-used, greatly worn and shabby, dog-eared copy of *The Complete Mother of the Groom: How to be Graceful, Helpful and Happy* (emphasis added) *During This Special Time* for a possible chapter on troubleshooting, Lacey ordered invitations, selected bridesmaids, their dresses AND the color, created a preliminary guest list, gathered menu choices and prices for the reception and finalized details with her florist! I felt like I was in a movie being played in fast-forward with me being the only character stuck in slo-mo!

My sister-in-law, Joan, had been a friend of Lacey's family for years. I called her, on the verge of tears, desperately seeking her advice!

"Joan!!! Everything is moving so quickly! Have you seen the invitations? They're not engraved! And . . . there's A PICTURE ON THEM! A PICTURE . . . IN FRONT OF THE KISSING STATUE BY THE MIDWAY!" I wailed.

"So . . . they're not engraved! What does that matter?" she asked with obvious amusement. "They really reflect the kids! They're fine! I think they're cute," she said, thinking that I'd be consoled.

"WHAT? Invitations aren't supposed to 'reFLECT' anyone; they're not supposed to be CUTE; they're supposed to be ELEGANT! They're supposed to be engraved on white, ivory or ecru FINE card stock stationery!" I insisted. "And did you know that she's NOT planning to register for ANY china, silver or crystal?" I lamented.

"Well . . . a lot of young people are opting not to do that. Life has gotten more casual, you know! Things have changed since we got married." Joan explained calmly, still amused.

"NOT REGISTER??? How are people going to select nice wedding gifts for them?" I gasped.

"O.K. Calm down. I'll talk to her," said Joan, and with that, we hung up.

A couple days passed before Joan called to report that she had spoken to Lacey and had urged her to register so that wedding guests could help them set up their new home. Lacey was not convinced that she wanted to prescribe an itemized list of things from which her guests should choose. She felt that it was impolite and rude to expect people to buy certain preselected items! Finally, Joan was able to persuade Lacey to reconsider. She explained that wedding guests WANTED to give the bride and groom something that the couple would like but would not purchase for themselves; that they EXPECTED to find an extensive list on file with the bridal registry! I was over-the-moon-ecstatic and forever indebted to Joan for her positive influence on Lacey! I had dodged a bullet without having to say one word to Lacey! This was proof that I knew how to keep my mouth shut! I had gotten my way -- pomp and circumstance prevailed! I had mastered Step 3: Keep Your Mouth Shut!

As soon as our phone conversation ended, I immediately jumped onto Lacey's bridal registry at Bed, Bath & Beyond's website, overjoyed to study her selections. It's a good thing, however, that my office chair not only had a high backrest, but also sturdy arm supports because as soon as my computer screen displayed the registry, my lungs crumpled, rendering me unable to breathe, I became light-headed and I knew I didn't have the strength to stand! Oh, Lacey had registered, all right, but she'd only requested two of each item: two plates, two coffee cups, two cereal bowls, two juice glasses, two wine glasses, two champagne flutes, two knives, two forks, two spoons, two of this, two of that -- as if she were loading The Ark by twos!!

Now, it happened that Drew and Lacey were coming over for dinner that evening, so I had only five or six hours lead time within which to compose myself and regain my strength! I simply could NOT believe that the bridal registry was so incomplete; I would have preferred no registry at all rather than one only Noah could appreciate!

The happy couple floated in on their cloud of love and happiness, giddy with excitement over the upcoming nuptials. We chatted about all the preparations and all the fanfare. I vehemently struggled internally about whether or not to broach the bridal registry issue, but finally decided to jump right in! (So much for Step 3!)

124

"Lacey," I began, clearing my throat for my words to flow, "Joan told me that you registered at Bed, Bath & Beyond."

"Oh, yes!" she sang, "I'm SO excited! You'll have to check it out!"

"Well -- as a matter of fact, I HAVE already!" I continued. "I love your choice of everyday dishes, especially the size and shape of the coffee mugs!" (I was rather proud of how well I'd achieved joy in my voice considering the great strain and stress ravaging my insides!)

"Thank you! I love them too!" she replied.

"But . . . " I cautiously continued, " . . . I'm just wondering why you only checked two of each item in the "Needed" column?"

"Oh! That's easy!" she answered, "one for me and one for Drew!"

O.K. We've got a starting point! You've opened the dialogue, now proceed with tact! Be very, VERY careful!

"Oh! That works . . . but . . . what about if you have a dinner party or if Michael and I come over for dinner? Should we bring our own place settings? Maybe we could leave them at your house so we don't have to bring them each time!" I suggested helpfully.

"<GASP!> Hey, Babe!" she called to Drew who was sitting in the adjacent family room, "We're going to have to update our registry!"

And with that, Lacey laughed and acknowledged that there were several other items she could add to the list. She even ASKED me to suggest some things!

Our evening together continued, and try as I may to scrutinize and peck at my ever-growing mental list of deviations from "proper wedding etiquette," I found myself genuinely charmed by Drew's fiancé. She cast a magic spell on me! She transformed me from Maleficent into Mary Poppins! My cold, hard shell cracked, shattered and fell to the floor in pieces. I recognized special qualities in her that caused me to reassess my rigid, inflexible, hoity-toity attitudes. Lacey is humble, completely unassuming, honest, funny, genuine, moral, and intelligent; and, she loves my son. Completely. Why should I hold firm to conventions that dictate five or six hours of a wedding day when it's grit and tenacity that hold a marriage together -- not china and silver and engraved invitations? Besides that, I took a mental inventory of all the sterling silver serving pieces I had stored in my dining room and I had to admit that many of them had never been used!

That's when Step 11 was conceived: Personify and embody those words on the plaque: "Be the Change You Want to See in the World (of mothers-in-law!)" I considered the direction my relationship with Lacey (AND Drew) would have gone had I continued to find fault. It didn't look pretty -- not pretty at all! In my mind's eye I was a wrinkled old woman dressed in dark colors -- head wrapped in an old, moth-eaten babushka and probably a wart on the end of my beak-like nose and a couple of grey, wiry hairs sticking wildly out of my pointed chin. Drew and Lacey trembled at the thought of having to visit me. They cowered in the corners of their life, miles and miles away from anywhere near me! Why would I want to begin that chapter of our lives with black resentment and judgment? Why not take the first step down the road less travelled and accept "what is" with joy? It just may be the first step toward a strong bond of friendship with your daughter-in-law! It may be that I could actually acquire a new friend! Wouldn't that be a 'win-win'?

Letting go of MY expectations and becoming willing to "live and let live" pulled a mountain of weight off of me! I felt as victorious as the last remaining contestant on The Biggest Loser -- not only for shedding the most weight, but also for gaining a brand new outlook on my future relationship with my son and his wife! It was I who'd changed, and it felt GREAT! Drew had chosen a mate and it was not MY place to superimpose MY preferences in their plans. Change may not always be easy, but in this case, it was worth it! I was disarmed of my preconceived expectations by allowing myself to be charmed by Lacey, my sweet new friend!

Step 12: Enjoy Your New Friendship with Your Daughter-In-Law

"There's not a word yet, for old friends who've just met!"

--Jim Henson

People drift across each other's paths throughout the course of their own lives. Childhood friends may grow apart as their interests develop and change. Perhaps a family moves away, severing an attachment through geographical distance. A new kid enters the classroom in sixth grade, longing to be accepted. New hires become part of the team at work. As Life continues, constant opportunities arise to become acquainted with many different types of people. There is no prescription for friendship; no age limit; no race or gender restriction. Friends become friends for a variety of causes and for a variety of reasons. When a son brings that special someone into your life, open your arms with a warm welcome for you may have just met an old friend.

Both Tim and Drew dated a lot of girls. Some I liked, some I tolerated and some I didn't like at all. Becoming friends with any of them, however, never blipped across my radar screen. Neither of my sons had as yet given any signs that they had found The One.

Tim had been out of college for a while, attending night classes at a local university to pursue an advanced certification in financial planning while working three jobs. He waited tables part time at a popular Italian restaurant near the beach as one of them. He invited me out one afternoon to sample the "best pizza in town." What I didn't know was that the invitation to pizza was just a rouse! He really wanted me to just happen to be in the restaurant so he could introduce me to a girl he liked. His plan backfired, though, because the girl had called in sick on that very day!

"C'mon, Mom, let's go for a ride," he said as he walked me to my car.

"Why? Where? What?" I asked, wondering what in the world was going on.

"I just want to show you this house around the corner. There's a girl I like who lives there," he explained.

"Oh my gosh! We're doing a drive-by?" I asked. "What if she's there?"

"Oh, she IS! She's sick today. I thought she'd be at the restaurant when you came in for pizza so you could meet her, but she called in sick," he said.

"So we're just gonna drive by her house? What if she peeks out the window and sees us? She's gonna think we're crazy or stalking her or something!" I protested, not wanted to do something I would have jumped at in high school.

"It'll be fine," Tim said, climbing into the driver's seat of my car. "Come on! I just want to show you where she lives!"

This behavior was so out of the ordinary, particularly for Tim, so I knew this girl was special. I still felt very childish driving past her house and just wanted to cruise by, drop my son back off at the restaurant, and go on my merry way. We turned off the main drag onto a residential side street. Tim slowed the car down to a snail's pace, then HONKED THE HORN!

"WHAT ARE YOU DOING?!" I whisper-screamed as I dove onto the floor of the passenger side. "I don't want her to see me gawking at her house! I've never even met her! She's going to think you've got a weird mother! In fact, she's going to think YOU'RE some sort of weird-o freak! Did you ever think of THAT?!"

I couldn't tell if Kristen peered out her window or not because of my stealth position curled up on the floor of the car, but I was already preparing my apology to deliver when I met her in person. I was SURE I would meet her . . . and soon.

Tim called to make arrangements to stop by our house on his way back from the desert the following weekend. Kristen would be with him, and he wanted to formally introduce her to my husband and me. We confirmed that the weekend would be fine and told him that we were excited to meet her. I was both anxious and excited all week long! In fact, I'll wager that I was more nervous about meeting Kristen than she was about meeting me! After all, this was the beginning of . . . of . . . Paul Stookey's lyrics coming true: ". . . a man shall leave his mother . . . and there is love."

Would she like me? What should I say? How should I act? Oh! I hope I don't embarrass Tim! Should I apologize to her for the "drive-by?" No! If I say something about it and she DIDN'T see us, then I'll have to tell her what we did! Aaaaauuuuuggggghhhh!

My fears proved to be all for naught. Tim and Kristen arrived at the house, and I liked her the minute I saw her. They only stayed for a short while, but I felt a comfortable easiness about her. I also saw a warm glow on my son's face that assured me that all was right.

Kristen came into my life through my son and I am very happy that she did. Our friendship is new, but I know that the roots will grow deep. She is someone I respect and someone with whom I enjoy spending time. I particularly like the times we have when it's just the two of us together. Friday mornings when I arrive at her house to babysit my grandson for the day, are special "talking times." We don't solve any of the world's problems or discuss any deep philosophical issues at all. We're just us. We talk about babies, child development, preschool, vaccinations, working versus not working and lots of other things that are important in new mothers' lives. I tell her what I did, mistakes I made along the way, regrets I have and goals that I accomplished. Kristen made me feel particularly validated by one of the birthday cards she and Tim sent me. It had a Superman emblem on the front. When I commented about it, Kristen said, "It's TRUE! You ARE a Super Woman! You had a full-time job, you were a single parent and you STILL managed to have a dinner on the table every night! I work part time and I have a hard time managing that!" Whether or not Kristen peeked out of her window the day of Tim and my infamous drive-by, I am SO grateful that she married my son!

My other new friend, Lacey, is someone that I believe my soul has known for a long, long time. Being with her is comfortable and easy. Drew first met her by accident -- or so I initially thought! While home from college over a holiday break, my brother-in-law invited Drew to work out with him early one morning. Tom and Steve, Lacey's father, always worked out in Steve's home gym that they'd dubbed the IHOP -- International House of Pain. Unbeknownst to Drew (and me), Tom and Steve schemed to have

Drew come to the house on the pretense of exercising, but they really planned to have him meet Lacey. Once Lacey understood the "plan," she exploded!

"NO THANK YOU, DAD!! I don't need your help finding boyfriends! I can't believe you think I'm so pathetic that you have to troll for a boy for me!" she roared.

And with that, she purposely made herself look as unattractive as possible to ensure that no boy would look twice in her direction and to teach her father to stay out of her love life! She pulled on a pair of her older brother's baggy basketball shorts and one of his worn and ragged jerseys; not even bothering to run a brush through her waist-length chestnut colored hair, she pulled it to the top of her head in an off-center ponytail. To finish the look, she chonked on a couple pieces of chewing gum, smacking it as she swaggered into the IHOP picking at her fingernails. The minute she laid eyes on Drew, however, she knew she'd made a terrible mistake! There he was, completely absorbed in his workout routine -- a perfect specimen of physical fitness (as are all Naval Academy midshipmen) -- pumping iron with the ease of Hercules! Lacey's jaw dropped so far that the gum in her mouth nearly fell out onto the floor! She gasped, then turned and ran from the gym, never to be seen for the rest of the morning! Her anger at her father blew to a whole new level!

"HOW COULD YOU DO THIS TO ME???!!!! YOU AT LEAST COULD HAVE TOLD ME THAT HE WAS GORGEOUS! YOU HAVE RUINED MY LIFE AND I WILL NEVER FORGIVE YOU!!!"

This scenario was relayed to me second hand via Joan, my sister-in-law. Both of us felt badly that Steve's well-intentioned efforts backfired and that Lacey was the one who was hurt. The holidays over, Drew returned to Annapolis until his next leave in April.

Apparently, Steve did not learn his lesson about interfering in his daughter's love life! Forever meddling and playing Cupid, Steve and Tom (the Dynamic Duo) pulled another arrow from Cupid's quiver and invited us to Tom and Joan's house for Easter dinner. Of course Steve, his wife Mary Louise and Lacey were invited also. This time, however, Steve let Lacey know that Drew would be there. Rather than being angry about her father's continued scheming, she was ecstatic about the "do over!"

"I spent the whole day getting ready," she told me a while ago, "I wanted to look as beautiful as I could possibly get!"

Whether the stars and planets were aligned or whether Cupid's arrow hit its target, Drew and Lacey's relationship began on Round 2. She and I met that Easter afternoon and continued to develop our friendship during the staged photo shoot vignettes we had while Drew was deployed to Okinawa. She has always welcomed me and has accepted me as a friend rather than just as Drew's mom.

Through the course of my sons' courtships, engagements, weddings and early years of their marriages, my self-study and concentration on being the best M.O.M.S. I can be has challenged me to accept this transition with a new perspective on my adult sons and my role in their lives. I am grateful for the courage I had to look inward and to adjust my attitudes. I believe that these twelve steps for Mothers of Married Sons will negate the old stereotype image of that dreaded old shrew of a mother-in-law.

M.O.M.S. -- UNITE!

Slogans from other 12-step programs that apply to **M.O.M.S.**

1. Easy Does It

2. First Things First

3. Live and Let Live

4. Think . . . think......think

5. One Day at a Time

6. KISS---keep it simple stupid

7. This Too Shall Pass

8. Expect Miracles

9. Do Not Complain

10. Be part of the solution, not the problem

11. Sponsors: have one-----use one-----be one

12. Keep an open mind

13. It works if you work it

14. Willingness is the key

15. You will be amazed

16. Don't quit 5 minutes before the miracle happens

17. Have a good day --- unless, of course, you have made other plans

18. It takes time

19. You are not alone

20. Count your blessings

21. Share your happiness

22. Respect the anonymity of others

23. Let go of old ideas

24. Take what you can use and leave the rest

25. Help is only a phone call away

26. Anger is but one letter away from danger

27. Courage to change

28. Before engaging your mouth, put your mind in gear!

29. M.O.M.S. is not something you join, it's a way of life

30. Give time . . . . time

31.   Resentments are like stray cats . . . if you don't feed them, they'll go away.

32.   In order to change the way we feel we must change the way we react.

33.   It's not old behavior if I'm still doing it.

34.   Without forgiveness, there is no future.

Made in the USA
San Bernardino, CA
22 August 2014